William O. Douglas

William O. Douglas

A Biography

by   EDWIN P. HOYT

Library of Congress Cataloging in Publication Data

Hoyt, Edwin Palmer.
  William O. Douglas.

  Bibliography: p.
  Includes index.
  1. Douglas, William Orville, 1898–   2. Judges—United States—Biography. I. Title.
  KF8745.D6H69   347′.73′2634 [B]   78–19868
  ISBN 0-8397-8598-4

9 8 7 6 5 4 3 2 1

Grateful acknowledgment is made to Random House for permission to reprint photographs previously published in *Go East Young Man.* Copyright © 1974 by William O. Douglas.

This book is for all who have ever hiked a trail, or climbed a mountain, or fished a sparkling stream, or wanted to; to remind them all that as we approach the 21st century there is still plenty of room for adventure in this world.

Contents

Preface

William O. Douglas has long been one of my personal heroes. Few men have been so fortunate, and so perspicacious as to establish trends in American history. Mr. Justice Douglas is one of those few.

Early in his career he espoused the cause of conservation, which later became known as "environmentalism." He was a good 30 years ahead of most of the rest of the country.

Moreover, the older Douglas grew in years, the younger he seemed to become in his approach to freedom. During the "frightened forties" he stood as one of that handful of men who were uncowed by the Communist witch hunt in America. He began in the '50s to press for an ever greater degree of libertarian philosophy in the law, while all around him lesser men were increasing restrictions on freedom.

As government has grown in America, a few men like Douglas have helped to prevent it from running over us all like a juggernaut. Year after year he and Mr. Justice Black and Mr. Justice Frankfurter stood, increasingly alone as the years passed, against the conservatism that was overtaking the nation and the U.S. Supreme Court.

This attitude has little to do with age; Mr. Justice White, one of the youngest justices, also has shown himself to be one of the most conservative. Nor is it a question of "liberalism" vs. "conservatism."

Douglas always called himself an old time "conservative" and in a sense he was that, espousing those conservative principles of the American Revolution: the conservation of the rights of man, and the conservation of the natural world in which he might exercise those rights.

Douglas has always believed, also, in the stringent application of the First Amendment to the U.S. Constitution, and has stood for the rights of reporters to pry, poke, and probe—although in his own life this probing has often been uncomfortable, many times unfair, and sometimes outrageous.

I have known Mr. Douglas ever since I was a small boy, when he and my father, then an Oregon newspaperman, used to set out from our house early of a morning, headed for a trout stream in the Oregon wilderness.

While I was a college student I was so deeply impressed with Mr. Justice Douglas's activities on the Court that I thought seriously about becoming a lawyer. The war cancelled all that out, and circumstance took me far afield from the law. But the impression was a serious one and lasting.

Early in the '40s I saw him in his judicial role in Washington. Late in the same decade, when I returned from foreign wanderings, I saw him again.

In later years, when I found myself engaged in writing a book on the 1930s, called *The Tempering Years,* Mr.

Justice Douglas helped me in unravelling the story of the Wall Street didoes of Richard Whitney.

And on a number of occasions when I visited Washington I would stop in at the Supreme Court to call on Mr. Justice Douglas, always to find him cheery, smiling, and looking out at the world with that pixy grin and untarnished enjoyment.

When I moved to Vermont, we had discussion of the enviable lot of Vermonters, and later of the leadership they showed in environmental affairs.

At one point I was engaged in a farming venture and a struggle (losing) to prevent the takeover of our little central Vermont town by flatland foreigners from New York and other big cities, and I received much aid and comfort in this rear-guard action from Mr. Douglas.

So the memories are many, and fond, and will be with me always.

William O. Douglas

1

The Wilderness

What occurred in the background and upbringing of William O. Douglas to make him such a lover of liberty, such a defender of freedom, such a man of the wide outdoors?

What William O. Douglas became was what he *had* to become, given the sort of background he had, his birthplace, the standards and values of those near and dear to him, and the workings of the American society on his character.

Douglas came from two staunch strains of the people who journeyed across oceans to America. On his mother's side, the names were Thompson, Fisk, and Bickford, hardy people who came to the wilderness of the "Hampshire Grants" in Vermont.

One of his forbears was Daniel Pierce Thompson, a Montpelier editor who became famous for his book on the Green Mountain Boys of Ethan Allen's day, those woodsmen who had captured Fort Ticonderoga from the British at the outset of the war of independence.

3

Vermont Fisks fought in the Civil War. They moved west seeking opportunity, to the country around Fergus Falls, Minnesota.

Orville and Salome Fisk, Douglas's maternal grandparents, settled in Maine, Minnesota, in the 1880s and established a farm where they grew wheat. Orville Fisk interested himself in government and the school board, and served both at times, once as county clerk.

Orville Fisk died at 41 and then the burden of the six children and the family farm fell on Salome.

On his father's side, Douglas was descended from a Highland Scot Douglas family, which had emigrated to Nova Scotia in the early days of the Canadian colonies and settled in Pictou Country, near the Middle River, not far from the Straits of Northumberland. The Douglases were Presbyterians.

Soon they had a town, Alma, and a Presbyterian Church. The land there was poor; later on, visiting Alma, Douglas would remark that it was "very close to starvation land."

These Douglases were farmers. They kept sheep and cattle and planted fruit trees. Alexander Douglas married Martha Archibald, and took her to live on a farm near Green Hill. There she bore a son, William Orville, and then shortly after that she died. Alexander married again, and the children of the two marriages grew up together.

William Douglas went to school in Alma, a one-room schoolhouse. In the 1880s he was sent to Pictou, where an academy had been established. At the academy, young Douglas acquired a fair education, and decided that he wanted to become a minister.

He headed south, to the United States, to Chicago, to attend the Moody Bible Institute. On April 6, 1898, the Reverend William Douglas was ordained at Crockton, Minnesota, and that spring he was ''called'' to the pastorate at Maine, Minnesota.

Pastor Douglas's job was anything but a sinecure. He lived in the parsonage at Maine and preached at the church there. He also had a church at Maplewood and one at Battle Lake. He preached two sermons on Sundays, and one on Thursday evenings, and he was responsible for the spiritual welfare of all three congregations.

In 1895, the Reverend Mr. Douglas met Julia Fisk, who played the organ in the church. She was a slight, auburn-haired girl. The young minister fell in love and asked Julia to marry him. They were married, and in 1897 a daughter was born, Martha Douglas. A year later, in 1898, a boy, William Orville Douglas, was born. The family called him Orville. Later, when the family had moved farther west, another son, Arthur, was born.

Soon after the birth of William Orville, the family headed south, to settle in Estrella, in San Luis Obispo County. They had travelled west by train to Oakland, then taking the ferry across San Francisco Bay.

William Orville was at least partially responsible for the family's move. He had contracted poliomyelitis in Maine, and for a time the family believed he would die. He recovered, but was partly paralyzed in the legs. His parents decided to take him to the warm, dry climate of California. Here Orville's health improved enough so that when he was six he could go to school.

His legs were still very weak. Every night his mother massaged them, and the massage seemed to help. So did the dry air of the Paso Robles country.

But again, Estrella did not suit the Douglas family. William's father could not bear the dry, hot summers. So after the third child, Arthur, was born, the family headed north.

They settled in at Cleveland, Washington, in the hills north of the great winding Columbia River that separates Washington and Oregon. It was a ranching area, known as Horse Heaven because of the fine grass and rolling hills.

This was "big sky" country, where men and women lived on "places" that might be six or seven thousand acres. Of course, it was mostly grassland, or planted in wheat, sometimes wheat where it should have stayed in grass—a fact of ecology that many a rancher would learn to his regret the hard way.

This western country, shortly after the turn of the twentieth century, was not unlike Vermont country had been in the days of young Douglas's grandparents, or Nova Scotia country in the youth of his father. The people did not have many material goods. They worked together, out of necessity.

If a man needed a new barn, he got his neighbors to help him build it. And when it came another's turn, he pitched in with a will to help build. Churches and public buildings were put up by people working together. The country was big enough that people did not step on one another's toes. A man who felt bound by the town could get away for a fishing trip easily enough, or a long ride in the countryside, where he was apt to see jackrabbits, deer, and other wild creatures and no humans.

Orville's father had as arduous a schedule here as ever. He preached in Cleveland, a village of a hundred people. He preached in Dot, a few miles south, and in Bickleton, a few miles east. He rode back and forth, attending the sick, burying the dead, preaching his sermons, attending to the welfare of this scattered flock.

The Reverend Mr. Douglas developed ulcers and he decided in the summer of 1904 to go for treatment to Portland, the nearest big city. The treatment for ulcers then involved hospitalization and surgery; the modern treatment of diet and medicines had not yet been developed.

So the Reverend Mr. Douglas journeyed down to Portland, and his wife accompanied him. The operation, they said, was a success. But in a few days, the patient died.

When Julia came back, desolated, she had to face a difficult situation. A new preacher was coming, and she must go.

But go where?

A minister's pay was very small and the Douglases were not independently wealthy—far from it. Julia Douglas could not even afford to return to Minnesota. Her older sister lived in Yakima, so she bundled the children up and settled down to make a new life there, with $2500, the proceeds from the life insurance the Rev. Mr. Douglas had taken out.

Mrs. Douglas spent $600 to build a five-room house in Yakima at 111 North Fifth Avenue.

By investing the $1900 remaining she might have

lived very frugally, but Mrs. Douglas fell into the hands of a lawyer who was careless with his clients' funds. He invested her money in a wild scheme for the development of desert lands east of Yakima. The project was a total failure—and Mrs. Douglas lost every penny.

So at six years of age, Orville Douglas knew real poverty, of the sort where even a child's earnings were prized—they sometimes meant the difference between eating and not eating.

The half-crippled young Orville Douglas cut the grass of neighbors' yards, and washed windows and ran errands. For a time he had a job sweeping out a store in the early morning. He learned to collect junk—old bags, and rags, and bottles, and sell them to the junkman of the town. In the summers the children picked berries, and cherries and peaches and apricots.

Douglas grew up in a strict religious atmosphere. He went to Sunday school in the early Sunday mornings, and then to church at 11. Late afternoon came the meeting of the young people's association, the Epworth League, and at 8 p.m. the evening church service. There was also the Thursday evening prayer meeting each week.

Soon Douglas began to detest the name Orville. It was a "sissy" name. He wanted to be called Bill, but until he left home years later, he was always Orville.

One of his greatest delights in Yakima was the nearness of the wilderness. When he was 11 years old, young Douglas began to go out camping. He went with other boys and their elders for nights at a time, to lie in a bedroll under the stars, and watch the big dipper as the clouds scudded by in the moonlight. He learned to know the sounds of wilderness night in the northwest, the hooting of the owls, the crackling of foxes and wild animals in the brush, the scrabbling of squirrels and chipmunks in the mist of early morning, the snorting of pegged-out horses, and their gentle whinnies. He learned to love the smell of bacon frying in a pan over a wood fire, and the taste of fresh-caught trout cooked in wood smoke, potatoes baked in ashes, and crayfish snared from under a rock.

He was on the lookout for cougars and bears and snakes and coyotes, but he saw few of them in these early years, until he learned more about the wilderness. The out-of-doors fascinated the small, thin child. The polio that had nearly cost him the use of his legs as a baby drove Douglas to seek the outdoors even more than most boys of his age, to strengthen himself.

In the course of self-treatment, Douglas learned about nature, and the world around him, not the world of technology and progress, but the immutable (it seemed then) world of animals, forests, and mountains.

As he grew older, he travelled farther, on more adventurous, more sophisticated trips. Eventually he would travel the world, into the heart of Asia and elsewhere, seeking, comparing, and learning.

2
William Orville Douglas and Equality

What William Orville Douglas learned in Yakima, besides an everlasting love for the out-of-doors, was the need for real equality of men. Rich and poor in these raw western towns seemed to be much alike. There was one school and everybody's children went there. It made no difference if your socks were new, or old and darned. As one of his teachers told him, it was what was up on top that counted. The boy saw no class distinction in Yakima —at first.

But as Douglas grew older he realized this his family was poor. It was a matter of having a Christmas tree with very little under it. It meant wearing clothes that came in a big Christmas box from the Presbyterian Mission. The Douglases accepted food and other gifts with no hope of reciprocating.

For eight years Douglas attended the Columbia Grade School and then he went to the local high school in Yakima. He did well, because it had been ingrained in him that he had to do well, and that education would bring release from the poverty that dogged the family.

There was very little in the way of casual labor in this small western town. The circus came around once a year, and like many a boy in many a town, he carried water for the animals, and helped the roustabouts when they would let him. He worked at the sideshows of the country fair, taking tickets.

In Orville Douglas's adolescent years the poverty became hard to take. Patched, second-hand, or worn-out clothes were an embarrassment. Because of this, Douglas developed an antipathy to the commercial idea of "Christmas" and "charity" that was never to leave him. On one particular occasion he received a handsome coat in one of the Christmas boxes. Much as he admired the coat, he would never put it on.

Men should be born and live with equal opportunity before them. Thus, in a small way, were the seeds of a young radical sown, a radical of a very common western type. One might say Douglas was a "populist." He decided that he would make of his life something of which he could be proud.

Young Douglas grew up a harum-scarum lad, so often the case with the sons of ministers. He and his cronies divided their world into friends and enemies. They rewarded their friends and punished their enemies. One of their favorite punishments for an enemy was to tip over his outhouse (preferably with him inside). But if young Douglas was a "roughneck," he was not an idle one. He worked whenever and wherever a boy could. He saved his pennies and bought a bicycle, and learned to ride it on the rough country roads.

When Douglas was 14 years old he saw his first president. Theodore Roosevelt came to town and made a speech in the station at Yakima from the back of his campaign train. T.R. spoke eloquently of the virtues of the Great Bull Moose, and the agonies of the Republican party, but young William Orville Douglas did not hear —he was much too far away from the platform. Nor was he interested. His T.R. was a big game hunter and "Rough Rider." President Roosevelt was a grave disappointment to a teenaged boy looking for glamor.

In those Yakima years Douglas learned oratory, and American history, with a heavy emphasis on the role of business in America. He became a proficient Latin student and by determination, something of an athlete—a long-distance runner and basketball player.

He was still Orville Douglas, still hating the name. He was painfully shy, but there was some quality about him that caused his fellow students to admire him. He graduated first in his class and was chosen valedictorian. Someone prophesied that one day Orville Douglas would be president of the United States.

His high standing brought him a scholarship to Whitman College, a small liberal arts school in Washington state.

By the time Orville Douglas was ready to go to college, he had learned a good deal about life. In the many jobs he had held, as newsboy, bowling alley pin-setter, and boy of the streets, Douglas learned that America, the "land of equality," was really a class society. Once a local do-gooder asked Douglas to spend Saturday and Sunday nights in the red light and saloon district. The honest citizen would pay Douglas a dollar a night to get women to solicit him, and bartenders to sell drinks to him. Then he was to give affidavits to the police. The authorities would move against the offenders. He was to help "clean up" Yakima.

For several weeks Douglas mingled with the poor, the tramps, the prostitutes, the down and out, and as he did so, he developed a sympathy for them and a distaste for the people who were trying to entrap them.

He also learned that while he was entrapping these people to "better society," his reform-minded employer was busy foreclosing mortgages, and cheating other businessmen.

Orville Douglas did not forget what he had seen. The young Douglas also had his heroes. One was Hiram Johnson, governor and senator from California, who fought the Southern Pacific Railroad and other baronial interests in behalf of the people. Another was William E. Borah, the senator from Idaho. Another was the great defender, Clarence Darrow.

If the boy Douglas had been given his choice of employment in his high school years, he said he would have become a forest ranger. One of his lasting heroes (who, he said, had more influence on him than all the others) was Gifford Pinchot, Theodore Roosevelt's Chief of the U.S. Forest Service and the leading conservationist of his time.

And still other heroes were members of the International Workers of the World. These people—called "Wobblies"—were mostly itinerants, often hoboes and sometimes revolutionaries whom Douglas encountered in his wanderings over the countryside outside Yakima. Sometimes Douglas went from place to place looking for a job. He got to know sheepherders and Indians, and dozens of others who lived close to the land and worked with their hands. He grew to love these people. Many years of life in cities would not wipe away these memories. Douglas would always have understanding and sympathy for "plain people." He saw in them love of life, the land, and freedom.

3

The Tools of His Trade

Just before the college semester began in the autumn of 1916, William Orville Douglas went to Walla Walla, 165 miles from Yakima, to enter Whitman College. His scholarship would pay the tuition of $100 a semester. But he would have to work his way to pay for board and room. Before he committed himself, he had to find a job.

He rode the rails to Walla Walla; his hobo friends had taught him the trick of riding the rods, and how to open an empty boxcar. When he got to Walla Walla, he got a job at Falkenberg's jewelry store. It paid 50 cents a day for five hours' work in the afternoon.

Douglas knew that was not enough money to support himself, so he got another job, as janitor in an office building and store, working in the morning. He found a third job as waiter in a cheap restaurant, which gave him two meals a day.

So the college student could arise before dawn, sweep out the office and store, go to classes in the mornings, "hash" at noon for two hours, work at the jeweler's until evening, wait tables again at dinner time, and then would be free to study until he was exhausted. It would be hard, but he was determined to get an education.

These jobs would make it possible for Douglas to send $20 a month home to his mother, and go to college at the same time. Altogether it seemed a most satisfactory future.

Douglas took the promises of employers and got on the train again (illegally) and rode back to Yakima. He picked up his bicycle there and then rode the 165 miles from his home to the college town.

Douglas had worked out all his problems except where to live. He solved that by pitching a tent near a brook on the edge of the campus. He lived there for several weeks. Then the college authorities caught up with him. What he was doing was illegal, they said. He must move into the dormitory.

That aspect of college life did not appeal to Douglas, for in these days freshmen were "hazed." They were not allowed to enter the main door of the campus buildings. They had to wear "dinks"—skullcaps that marked them as "green." They were sometimes abused physically, thrown into the brook or a pond on the campus. They were paddled for "offenses" against upper classmen. Douglas was far more mature than his years. He found the hazing senseless and irritating.

One night hazers nailed Douglas's shoes to the floor of his room while he slept. That was the last straw. He moved out of the dormitory, into the house of the Beta Theta Pi fraternity, as a "pledge," seeking full membership. Later, after he left the campus, Douglas rejected fraternities as clannish and snobbish, but at Whitman, he was happy enough in the Beta Theta Pi house.

During that freshman year at Whitman the United States declared war on the Kaiser's Germany. In the war fever that swept the campus Douglas decided to enlist. He went to the recruiting office to join the U.S. Marines. When he got there he saw a poster advertising naval aviation. He tried to enlist for aviation training, but he failed the color test. He went home to practice, picking out hanks of yarn of various colors. He never did get the red right. That was the end of his naval career.

He applied for Army Officer's Training School. He was supposed to take the color test again, but he managed to wiggle out of it, and passed the physical. He was in the Army.

Private Douglas was sent to the Presidio at San Francisco and then ordered right back to the ROTC unit at Whitman college. Later he was ordered to Camp Taylor, Kentucky for training in artillery school, but the Armistice was signed just then and the war was over. He went back to college.

Douglas continued a hectic pace, running from job to class, to job and back again. He did little but work; there was virtually no time for girls, or for movies or other entertainment. It was study and work, work and study, and when he joined the college debating team he found that he seldom got more than a few hours' sleep a night.

This hurried life held so many disappointments that later, when Douglas married and had children, he vowed that not one of them would ever have to work a day in college. It was not a question of feeling inferior to the wealthier students. In no sense did William Orville Douglas feel inferior. But he would have liked more leisure.

He was an idealist—a dreamer. He helped organize the Woodrow Wilson Club, dedicated to the principles of Wilson's "better world" through international cooperation. He believed thoroughly in the League of Nations as a means of preventing future wars. He examined religion, and found it wanting in most respects in spite of the large doses he had taken as a young boy. He believed in God, and Jesus Christ, but not in Christ's divinity, or the Holy Ghost or the resurrection of the body. This attitude toward religion, the right of people to believe what they would, but not to press it upon their fellow men, was to color many a Douglas decision in judicial years to come.

Altogether, college for Orville Douglas was a more serious time than it was for many of his contemporaries. He had learned early that education was a tool with which he could forge ahead in the world. He did not know quite how. His ideas were quickly formed and as quickly changed. He was easily influenced, and two of his professors impressed him deeply. One was a teacher of geology and sciences, and the other, a teacher of English.

He believed that Russia was going to be important to the world after the Communist revolution. He sought someone to teach him Russian, but could not find any one in Walla Walla to do so. He bought a grammar and tried to study alone. It was a dismal failure as an educational experiment. Years later when he visited the USSR he could scarcely remember a word.

His grades were excellent, his skills considerable, when in the spring of 1920 he graduated from Whitman College. He was 20 years old and ready to challenge the world.

4
Go East, Young Man,
for Opportunity

When young William Orville Douglas left the sheltered
environment of Whitman College (not that it had ever
sheltered him very much), his mother was still having
financial problems. His sister Martha had delayed her
education so Orville could have his, and his brother
Arthur was about to start college.

The responsibility for helping his mother fell on the
shoulders of the young graduate. He found a job at
Yakima High School teaching English, public speaking,
and Latin. He also picked up other odd jobs, including
one teaching part time at a one-room schoolhouse in
nearby Wiley City.

In the Wiley City school, the eight classes were divided according to student size and age, with the little
ones up front and the big ones in the back. Keeping
order in such a schoolhouse was difficult. The teacher
had to teach one class, with his eye on seven others—
and particularly the last three grades, where the "hell-
raisers" usually appeared.

One big boy from the 8th grade decided he would challenge the new young teacher. He began deliberate provocation. Douglas warned the boy that he would not tolerate rowdyism. When the boy attacked him, Douglas subdued him. The boy went away from school, vowing vengeance.

The next morning he showed up with his father, a bigger bully than the pupil. The father announced that since teacher Douglas had laid hands on his boy he was going to whip the teacher.

Thereupon Douglas was forced into a fight. He battered the other man until the father said he had had enough, and then Douglas went back to teaching the class. He had no more trouble with that 8th grade bully, nor with any other pupils.

Such an incident would have been almost unheard of in the East in those days; certainly in Scarsdale or Manhasset or Arlington. But this was big sky country; the West was still woolly and wild, and the sort of independence (even violence) that would put a man in jail in the East would go virtually unnoticed out near the Cascade Range. Nobody called the sheriff; no more was said. The law of the West was not the law of the East.

Yakima was a seat of considerably higher cultural activity than Wiley City. For two years Douglas taught at Yakima, an experience that dampened his ardor for English, Latin, and public speaking, although the young teacher was soon coaching the debating squad. He led his debaters to the state championship. He also developed a certain bitterness, because he had applied for a Rhodes Scholarship, and learned that he really did not have a chance against the élite sons of good family from Seattle and Tacoma who wanted the appointment. He tried, he failed; he knew that the failure was built into the system, and it made him a little more rugged, a little more disinclined to accept the society around him.

At this same time, Douglas was having other hard lessons. He joined the American Legion—natural enough for a former soldier after World War I, for the Legion was a soldier's club.

But Douglas soon found that he could not stomach the legion's politicization; the organization came out against Orientals, for restriction of "Bolsheviks" and in favor of a sort of police state to be managed by the Department of Justice. Douglas did not believe in police states. He let his Legion membership lapse. It was not to be renewed.

In order to earn more money, Douglas tried selling insurance. The experiment was not successful, but he made friends with the agent, O.E. Bailey, and Bailey introduced the younger man to new ideas about the law and the courts. They discussed the need for political and judicial reform. Bailey had actually visited the U.S. Supreme Court and he had many tales to tell. Soon young Douglas was visiting the courtrooms of Yakima, attending trials to see how justice actually worked.

Over the months the law became his major interest. In spite of the opposition of his mother, who wanted him to remain with her in Yakima, he decided to study law. In the spring of 1922 Douglas applied to Harvard Law School for admission—and was accepted. Only then did he learn that because he was poor life was going to be very difficult for him in Cambridge. While worrying, he also met a recent graduate of Columbia University Law School, who gave him letters of introduction, including one to Dean Harlan F. Stone. Douglas believed there was a better atmosphere for him at Columbia and decided to go there instead.

In September, 1922, Douglas was ready to head east. He had saved $75 from his teaching. He had letters to prominent lawyers in the East which he hoped would open doors which he needed opened, in order to work his way through law school.

He got an assignment to take a flock of 2000 sheep to Chicago via the Great Northern Railway. He would ride the caboose to be on hand just in case something happened. In Chicago he would supervise the unloading at the stockyards.

The young man from Yakima was heading east, to cast his lot with the sophisticated Atlantic coastal community. He was deserting his rugged Western homeland. It did not come easily. As the train pulled out across the desert land of eastern Washington, Douglas felt like turning back. He was heading into the unknown, against his mother's wishes, without friends. But counteracting this yearning was an intense desire for success in America. He sensed that his key to that success lay in the East.

The whole venture nearly collapsed before the train left the state of Washington. Railroad workers, many of them radicals, struck all the American railroads just as Douglas set out on his journey and the train stopped in the wilderness. Douglas began buttonholing railroad employees to tell them that unless his sheep were fed and watered, they would die. The railroad would have a suit on its hands and the railroad would hold the strikers responsible. After many pleas, Douglas finally got through to authority—and up came a switch engine to take the livestock to a switching point which had pens for feeding and watering. The sheep were saved.

The labor troubles were sporadic in the railroads. The journey across country lasted weeks. Douglas and his sheep went to Miles City, Montana, and stopped. They moved on to Williston, N.D., and were sidetracked. They hit Minot and were stalled. Douglas had to take his sheep into the countryside to graze. On the way back one old ewe escaped, ran down the main street of Minot, and led her amateur shepherd a merry chase. But finally the job was done, and the sheep were delivered, not to Chicago, but to Minneapolis.

That was the end of Douglas's free ride east. He had run out of money on the long journey, so he decided to ride the rods. He was caught and thrown off a freight as it was moving, just outside Chicago. On the edge of the yards he found a "hobo jungle" and made friends with the hoboes. Here he got some good advice: watch out for railroad "bulls." In a city, stay out of flophouses; they will "roll" you there and take your money. Go to the YMCA.

Douglas listened and learned to survive. But by the time he reached New York City, riding freight cars, he had only six cents left.

In New York City he suddenly remembered Beta Theta Pi was a national fraternity which meant it had chapters in many cities. The "brothers" were bound to help one another. He went to the Beta Theta Pi house near Columbia University, encountered an old Whitman friend, and borrowed $75 from him.

But even so, the assault on the Eastern establishment nearly failed. Douglas did not have enough money to pay his tuition or his rent in the dormitory. The university authorities were about to eject him, when quite by chance he found a job. A businessman downtown in Manhattan told a law student that he wanted someone to teach him law. Douglas soon found out that what the man wanted was to have help in teaching law for a correspondence course he conducted and Douglas got the job. He also got a contract for $600, which paid his fees, and put him in good standing with the university, for that first year.

He had time to maneuver and find his way.

Douglas spent the next six years in New York as student, lawyer and teacher. But he never overcame his love for the mountains and the wilderness. He found eastern city people hard, and difficult for a westerner to stomach. New York City itself was sooty and miserable; he saw that even trees found it a struggle to survive in the shadows of the steel and concrete mountains. The longing for his beloved Cascade Range was strong. But he resisted homesickness. He still believed opportunity was here in New York.

During those years Douglas lived simply and cheaply. Much of the time he ate in Horn & Hardart's inexpensive Automat restaurants.

At Columbia Douglas met people, some distinguished, some to be distinguished. One classmate was Paul Robeson, the black athlete who would be a world famous actor and singer. Another was Thomas E. Dewey, who would be a Republican politician, governor, and candidate for president. Douglas got to know wealthy practicing lawyers and people of the business world. He also met the poor and miserable in New York's streets.

Douglas's social conscience drove him to take a job in a settlement house on Henry Street in downtown Manhattan. There he organized boys into a hiking and outing club. On weekends, he took the boys out of the city. They hiked into Rockland County, up the Hudson River. They went swimming in New Jersey. They studied nature in the Connecticut woods. Douglas needed the trips as much as the boys. He must have release from a life in the city that was so demanding intellectually, but so frustrating physically for a man of the outdoors.

Except for his settlement activities, Douglas worked almost all the time. Once he went to the opera. The opera could not compare to a sunset looking westward from a mountain top. He never went to another performance. Occasionally he went to the theater, to see the Ziegfeld Follies, and other entertainment. But he never acquired a taste for the amusements of New York.

He earned some money tutoring other students at Columbia. At the end of his first year in law school, Douglas was elected to the Columbia Law Review, a reward for superior grades. Sometimes, however, in the struggle for good grades, he came a cropper, as with a professor named Thomas Reed Powell.

Douglas had developed a high opinion of himself and his abilities, and usually his grades seemed to justify it.

In Professor Powell's course in constitutional law he submitted what he considered to be a first-rate paper. Professor Powell read it and gave him a C. Douglas was stunned and unhappy, until he learned that a number of other bright students had also been given Cs. Powell had a habit of bringing bright young men down to reality. It was hard to laugh about it during law school years, but later Douglas and several others got together to form a club called the Powell C Club, which celebrated their low grades. All members had achieved high honors in their profession.

In 1924, Dean Harlan Stone, of the law school, went to Washington to become attorney general in the cabinet of President Calvin Coolidge. Then, in 1925, after Associate Justice McKenna of the U.S. Supreme Court died, Stone was appointed to take his place.

The new U.S. Supreme Court justice decided that each year he would take a man from Columbia University Law School to be his clerk. Such an appointment was a key to success in the legal world. The law clerks of the nine justices were marked men. Usually they clerked for a year. Then, no matter where they went they found ways cleared for them.

William Orville Douglas aspired to the Stone appointment in the year of his graduation. He was at the top of his class, and a logical candidate. But Douglas was beaten out for class leadership in his senior year by a fellow student, Alfred McCormack. Mr. Justice Stone chose McCormack and not Douglas to be his law clerk in the coming year.

Douglas had already planned his future: he would go

to Washington for a year, mingle in the sanctified halls of the court with great names and fine minds, and then he would go home to Washington's big sky country to practice law. He already had an offer of a partnership in a firm in Walla Walla.

The failure to get the Stone appointment changed Douglas's plans. By the time Douglas graduated from Columbia, he had married Mildred Riddle, a young woman from Oregon he had met when they were both teaching at Yakima High School. In the last days of his student years he taught in schools around New York to support them.

Douglas felt the need to achieve success in the East. He joined the others of his class, then, to go around to New York law offices, seeking a connection. He was interviewed by John Foster Dulles, later U.S. secretary of state and an important corporation lawyer. Dulles impressed Douglas as drab, pompous and pontifical.

The dislike must have been mutual. No offer was forthcoming.

Douglas passed the Bar examination in New York that year. There had never been any question about that in his mind. Douglas pounded the pavements and finally was asked to join a big downtown corporation-law firm. He also was appointed to teach three courses at Columbia—an honor for a new law-school graduate. He got up early in the morning, rushed to Columbia to teach, and then caught the subway downtown to get to the law office by 9:30. It was more of the old life—learning and earning on the run.

In the downtown law firm he shared a tiny cubicle

with another lawyer named John J. McCloy, who would later become a government official, U.S. high commissioner in Germany at the end of World War II, and a powerful figure in the U.S.

This was the sort of ambience that New York offered; this was why Douglas had come to the big city.

5

The Hard Decision

Lawyer William Orville Douglas worked hard. Many a
night he stayed at the William Street offices until mid-
night. He was a corporate lawyer, working in a corporate
law firm, and not liking it very much. One of his tasks
was to attend stockholders' meetings. He carried with
him a briefcase filled with "proxies"—the votes stockholders who did not wish to attend a meeting gave to
others to vote on issues taken up at the meeting. Somehow the management of the corporation always seemed
able to get most of the proxies. To Douglas it seemed a
put-up job. The management of big corporations was
self-perpetuating. Dissenters always seemed to be
squelched. Douglas wondered then, why the corporate
system could be so easily manipulated by a handful of
people.

In those New York days Douglas became good friends
with his old law school classmate, Thomas E. Dewey.
They talked about forming a law partnership. But Douglas decided against it. He had the feeling that Dewey

33

really wanted to become a politician. Dewey did, a few years later going to the U.S. attorney's office in New York. He then won election as district attorney of New York City.

He gained fame by prosecuting gangsters, and won the governorship of New York. Finally Dewey ran for president in 1944 and 1948 on the Republican ticket.

Politics did not interest Douglas, although he learned a good deal about New York's elections. He was a special deputy attorney general, serving during New York city elections. He went to the polls as a watcher, to be sure that political machines did not try to vote tombstones. Tammany Hall was infamous for voting lists of the dead, and people who never existed. The record of that corruption went back nearly a century.

During one election, Douglas was assigned to a polling place on the lower East Side. He spent the whole day there, checking credentials and watching voters, trying to make sure that the polling was honest.

Late in the afternoon a number of young men suddenly came to his polling place. There was something about their appearance that told Douglas they were not legitimate voters. They were much too well dressed. They all seemed to know one another. Douglas challenged them. Where were their credentials? Credentials? One of the men shoved a gun in his ribs. There were their credentials! Douglas stepped back and said nothing as the "voters" cast their Tammany ballots. Then they went away, together, to the next polling place. Douglas said nothing to anyone. He had learned about Manhattan politics.

This experience strengthened Douglas's distaste for city life. So did the brutality of New York police. In the days in the West, when Douglas had been riding in the boxcars and "on the rods," he had encountered tough "railroad bulls" who beat up riders, or shot at them. New York police had the same attitude, he found. They were brutes in a brutal city.

At the end of the year, Douglas's friend in Walla Walla said he could not wait any longer for a decision. He needed a partner and he would have to take someone else if Douglas would not come immediately. Douglas let the chance go by, with misgivings. He stayed on in New York for another year.

In the second year, Douglas earned $3,600, which was a good salary for a young lawyer. If he stayed on long enough to become a partner he might earn $25,000 a year or more. But the money did not mean that much to Douglas. He did not like the work or the city life. He decided to leave. When the partners learned about his decision they offered him $5000 a year. But the smell of the mountains was strong in Douglas's nostrils. He held to his decision. Money would not keep him in the city he detested.

There was another reason for Douglas's dissatisfaction. He did not like the opera. He did not like many of the people he met at New York's glittering parties. He did not like formal clothes and formal balls. He found a vast difference between his views and those of the rich and powerful with whom his associates mingled. He shared practically none of their views on life or the uses of money.

He headed west, then, dreaming of dryfly fishing, of climbing a mountain and seeing the gleaming vista of a sunset spread before him, of tramping through a fresh field after a rain. He did not want—he did not believe he wanted—the sort of success in life that Wall Street law practice would offer him. He wanted the open life of the West.

He had no job nor many prospects. He went to Seattle, the biggest city in the Northwest. He could practice in the city, yet be within hours of the outdoors. He soon found that New York references did not impress Seattle lawyers, who resented easterners in general. The best offer made to Douglas was a promise of $50 a month as a law clerk. He gave up the idea of western-city practice, and decided to become a country lawyer. He went then to his own home town of Yakima to join the firm of James Cull.

Douglas settled down to the life of a small-town lawyer. His days were spent drawing mortgages on chicken coops, preparing wills, working up property deeds. After six months, he discovered he was earning $25 a month in legal fees, less than he had made as a college boy doing odd jobs. Life would have been impossible if he had not had savings from the New York years. He drew on his savings until they were nearly gone.

Somehow his mountains and fishing streams did not seem so attractive. Everything was overshadowed by his concern about making a living. His wife wanted to have children. How could he support children on $25 a month? When an offer came from Columbia University Law School for an assistant professorship that would pay

$5000 a year, it did not take Douglas long to decide that he should accept it.

This time, he was going back to a place he knew and disliked, but he was going back for a purpose. He was returning to the main stream of American life, which, he saw, was in the East. The longings of the past had worn thin in the cold light of reality. His old wilderness was the same, but he was not. Again, he set forth for the East to find what he was looking for.

Father and paternal grandparents of William O. Douglas. William Douglas, *above*; Alexander Douglas and Martha Archibald Douglas.

Cleveland, Washington, last pastorate of Douglas's father

William O., Arthur, and Martha with their mother, Julia Fisk Douglas, shortly after death of their father.

Yakima Avenue, 1908

William O. Douglas, *right*, with sister
Martha and brother Arthur.

Julia Douglas
with the night's dinner.

The Yakima High School basketball team. *Left to right*: Leo Nicholson, Tommy Pickering, Orville Douglas, Arthur Darby, Bradley Emery.

In the wilderness with a friend, about 1913

6

A New Sort of Teacher

Assistant Professor William Orville Douglas arrived at
Columbia University at a time when part of the Eastern
law community was changing its outlook. A group of
professors at Columbia University Law School had decided that the law as practiced was not serving the social
ends of America. They saw the law as a force for social
change.

Douglas's background of poverty, his observations of
the seamy sides of life, and his incompatibility with the
rich and powerful drew him to this group of dissidents.

These ideas of "socializing" the law were anathema
to the old school. Many practicing lawyers called this
approach "dangerous radicalism." Soon the young radicals frightened the traditionalists of Columbia. Nicholas
Murray Butler, president of the university, decided to
quell the incipient rebellion. He appointed a new law-
school dean without consulting the "young lions." The
new dean was a traditionalist in every way. Douglas was
furious. Further, he knew that he could not adjust to the

dean's ways of teaching. He resigned his post. It was 1928, and the young rebel was out of a job again.

What to do? He had an apartment in Pelham, a suburb of New York not far from Columbia University. He had hoped to make enough money in his work to buy a house for his wife and family. But how could he manage this in the unfriendly East?

As he was pondering, an old friend in eastern Oregon heard of his plight and offered him a law partnership. Once again the West was calling him back. Then, one day in May, at a dinner, he met Robert M. Hutchins, then dean of the Yale University Law School. Hutchins was a man of Douglas's own type. He was only in his twenties, but he was regarded as one of the most brilliant teachers in America. He was also a man of action. He liked Douglas, and respected what he knew of him. Next morning Douglas had a telephone call: Hutchins had arisen, called a "rump session" of the Yale law faculty —and they had elected William O. Douglas to become a member of that faculty.

And thus in September, 1928, Douglas became an associate professor of law at Yale University.

The Douglases moved to New Haven and began to raise a family. Their daughter Millie was born in 1929. Their son William was born in 1932.

Douglas was happy in New Haven. The university was truly a "haven" of intellectual freedom.

Under Robert Hutchins, Yale Law School of the 1920s and 1930s became a center of experiment. Many ideas were thrown out to challenge tradition. Hutchins himself introduced the idea of teaching a course in Evidence with a psychiatrist. The psychiatrist questioned the old rules of law. Thurman Arnold was teaching at Yale, and writing his *Folklore of Capitalism,* a book that would challenge many of the ideas of the capitalist society the United States had become.

Douglas joined in such ideas eagerly.

He had time to study, and the leisure to tramp in the Connecticut woods. It did not have the grandeur of the Western wilderness by far, and yet rural Connecticut was very pleasant.

In the beginning, Douglas was not a popular teacher at Yale. He did not like "spoiled brats," and Yale was full of them, young men, the sons and grandsons of Yale men, representatives of those families that had held wealth and power for generations. They were youths growing into the sort of people he detested. All around him, Douglas saw professors handling these youngsters with kid gloves. He decided to do just the opposite. He became hard and sarcastic in class. He dressed down students and humiliated them. The animosity between students and teacher became so pronounced that it colored the whole of his teaching. One day he was called in to Dean Hutchins's office. The dean informed him that a committee of students had come in demanding that Douglas be fired.

All right, Douglas said. He did not care if Hutchins wanted to fire him.

Hutchins smiled. That was not quite what he meant. If Douglas wanted to bear down harder on these children of privilege it was all right with him.

Robert Hutchins was as much an educational revolutionary as Douglas. They believed that education should serve society, that the law should most certainly be turned to serve society better than it was doing in the 1920s. America was the land of the economic royalist. Too many lawyers either were of that group or were their servants. They grew fat and rich by doing the bidding of the fat and rich. There were, of course, exceptions. Douglas had known some of these men by reputation in his Western years: the Borahs, the Johnsons, and the Darrows. Men who thought more of principle than of treasure.

But in the East he saw all that he did not like. He and Hutchins spent many long evenings discussing the problems of education, law, and society.

Douglas told Hutchins he was not even certain that he wanted to continue in the law, or that his decision to leave literature had been very intelligent.

But Douglas was still shy, and although he held highly liberal, even radical social ideas, he was anything but a Bohemian. His code of conduct was that of the son of a Baptist minister. One evening he invited the writer Sherwood Anderson to his house for a cocktail party, and when Anderson stubbed out a cigarette on his wallpaper and threw the butt on the carpet, Douglas called him a boor.

As a teacher Douglas was dedicated and hard working. He taught five hours a week. For each course he prepared for eight hours before teaching. Unlike many professors, he did not teach any course the same way twice. He never kept notes. He started out fresh each semester to explore the subject from a new aspect with his students.

Douglas was also an innovator. He and a professor at Harvard Business School put together a course of study in "business law." A student could earn both a law degree and a business degree.

Douglas believed in sending students out into the field to see how the law operated in fact rather than in theory. Abe Fortas, who later was to have a distinguished law career and become a Supreme Court justice, was one of Douglas's best students. Under Douglas, Fortas made a study of loan sharks and consumer credit. Douglas taught about what affected the average man, not what affected the very rich.

Speaking engagements and other activities often took Douglas from New Haven to Boston, New York, and Washington. For a time he conducted a bankruptcy clinic in New York. After the 1929 Wall Street crash, bankruptcies became so common that President Herbert Hoover asked William Donovan, a prominent attorney, to investigate bankruptcy.

Donovan knew that Douglas knew more about bankruptcy than most lawyers. He asked for help. In this task Douglas had his first taste of government. He travelled to Washington to work with Julius Klein, secretary of commerce in the Hoover cabinet.

Then came the election of 1932, and the victory of Franklin Delano Roosevelt that would change the life of William Orville Douglas.

7
The Securities
and Exchange Commission

Long before William Orville Douglas met Franklin D. Roosevelt, the new president was one of his particular heroes. Douglas knew what it had meant to him to have had polio, and the years he had spent walking, running, moving about the mountains and the river valleys, strengthening the legs that were only mildly affected by the disease, as compared to Roosevelt's.

And knowing that the elder man had been stricken as an adult, Douglas appreciated the effort Roosevelt had made to rebuild a shattered career. Douglas would not embarrass his hero by mentioning this, and although later he became a member of FDR's "poker-playing crowd"—a part of the inner circle—Douglas never told FDR about his own affliction with polio as a boy.

As a registered Democrat in Connecticut, Douglas began to take an interest in party politics.

He worked for Frank Maloney, who was running for the U.S. House of Representatives, and when Maloney was elected, this gave Douglas an important friend in a high place. Soon, Maloney was elected to the Senate.

The Roosevelt administration set out to discover the causes of the great crash of 1929, and to take steps to prevent such "panics" in the future. President Roosevelt appointed Joseph P. Kennedy, a Boston millionaire businessman, to be chairman of the Securities and Exchange Commission which would police the stock markets of the U.S.

Early in 1933, Kennedy was organizing this agency. He was concerned about groups of lawyers and businessmen that seemed to be manipulating the bankruptcy laws to their own ends. Kennedy learned that Douglas was an expert on bankruptcy, so he asked a mutual friend to see if Douglas would join the staff of the agency. Douglas accepted gladly. Here was a chance to put his theories into action.

Douglas secured a semester's leave of absence from Yale Law School, and went to Washington, not even taking his family. Why uproot Mildred and the children when he was going down only on a temporary assignment? It was much simpler to commute home to New Haven for weekends.

Soon he had an office, a secretary, and an assistant—his former student Abe Fortas. Several other bright young lawyers who had recently graduated from the best law schools joined his staff.

The temporary job dragged on. At the end of the semester, Douglas's group was deeply involved in investigation of the practices of the financial community, and he did not want to quit. The law school extended his leave of absence.

In Washington, Douglas and his staff worked long hours. Day after day he went to the Capitol for hearings. They lasted from 9 to 5, with a break for lunch. But evenings and early mornings were spent in preparation. He and his assistants worked late nearly every night.

Sometimes the hearings took them far from Washington. He encountered John Foster Dulles again. He saw other important corporation lawyers. He did not like them any better than he had before.

Once an investigation took him into the activities of Senator Burton K. Wheeler of Montana and earned him the enmity of Wheeler.

He stepped on more toes. He was not seeking success. He was attempting to sort out the affairs of a financial community that was not notable in the early 1930s for high moral standards in the conduct of business. Dulles, for instance, Douglas believed was the sort of man who would do anything for a fee, and then justify it by a "holier-than-thou" attitude.

In this period of his life, Douglas again faced the economic difficulty that he had thought had ended with his appointment at Yale. His SEC pay was $10,000 a year, but it cost him more than that to keep two households. He could survive only by borrowing money. He borrowed because he believed in what he was doing.

Douglas's unawed badgering of the community of big business brought the young law professor to the favorable attention of President Roosevelt. The president was amused by this irreverent young westerner who attacked the most important business leaders in America so effectively. The president had little respect for Wall Street;

the rich called him "a traitor to his class." He backed the investigation of big-business methods and he watched Douglas's activity and growth with sympathetic interest.

Soon Douglas was accepted into the second circle of the Democratic administration in Washington. Joseph Kennedy was close to Roosevelt and Douglas became close to the Kennedy family. He often visited the big Kennedy house in Maryland on SEC business, and he often stayed for dinner. He came to know all the Kennedys very well.

That friendship was the key to Douglas's next success. In 1935 Joseph Kennedy left the SEC, and James Landis (another friend of Douglas's from Columbia Law School days) was appointed chairman. But Kennedy still had influence and when another vacancy opened on the Securities and Exchange Commission, Kennedy suggested to Roosevelt that he knew the man to fill it: William Orville Douglas.

He said Douglas had all the qualifications. He was bright, young, accomplished, experienced in the work— and a good Democrat. The president was impressed. He appointed Douglas to the post, and he was confirmed by the United States Senate in January, 1936.

Yale gave Douglas another leave of absence, and he settled deeper into Washington.

The SEC was not a glamour agency, but its work was vital in the straightening out of the country's financial structure.

In the course of investigation of the methods of the business community, the SEC found that Richard C.

Whitney, president of the New York Stock Exchange, had illegally manipulated stocks and bonds for his own benefit. He was tried, convicted, and sent to prison. That case rocked the financial community. The SEC, then, did acquire a certain glamour, as the policeman of Wall Street, and Douglas and his staff gained prominence.

In these years the SEC established a whole new set of rules to prevent securities manipulation. The work led to passage by Congress of effective laws to prevent the swindling and sharpering that had been commonplace in America since the establishment of the stock exchanges.

For the first time, the federal government began regulation of the sale of securities, and regulation of exchanges and brokers. It broke up holding companies.

What was done was extremely complicated, but the results were to make a responsible financial community, and restore public trust in the business world.

Douglas gained a reputation as a liberal in his crusade for public participation in governing business. He wanted appointment of "public" directors of the biggest corporations like U.S. Steel and General Motors—people who represented the broad base of the American people rather than narrow business interests.

Such ideas were so far ahead of their time that they were not accepted by Congress.

One major accomplishment of the SEC in Douglas's days was the cleanup of the utilities system. In the late 1920s such men as Samuel Insull had created vast public utility empires. They bought control of utility companies. Then they "watered" the stock, issuing large amounts of new stock without increasing the company's assets. They then sold off the stock, and got out of the company with a huge profit, leaving the other stockholders to hold the bag.

The actions of these "utilities barons" were particularly obnoxious because they preyed on widows and orphans and retired people. Utilities securities were said to be the safest in the U.S., so many people with a little money put their savings into the "safe" investment. After the crash of 1929, dozens of these utilties companies went bankrupt or were reorganized. And when the values were assessed, many of the "little people" found their savings had been wiped out.

When the SEC came to investigate the utilities companies, Douglas and his associates found themselves locking horns with the largest and most important Wall Street law firms. John Foster Dulles became their particular enemy in this fight.

The years were filled with controversy. At one time Douglas faced some 200 court actions brought against the SEC by Dulles and other attorneys who were trying to stop Federal control. Douglas went up to Capitol Hill to buttonhole senators, to get them to rescind approval of certain legislation that would have benefited the financiers and hurt the public. Senator Hugo L. Black of Alabama was most helpful to him then.

Eventually, through a number of Supreme Court decisions, the SEC beat back Dulles's attempts to keep the utilities companies from falling under federal regulation.

In 1937 Douglas was elected dean of the Yale University Law School, after Hutchins went to the University of Chicago. Douglas had to think about his career then.

Should he go back there and spend his life teaching?

As he was pondering he learned that SEC Chairman James M. Landis was scheduled to go back to Harvard Law School. Douglas decided he would stay in Washington only if he was made chairman of the SEC. It did not seem that President Roosevelt was going to appoint him, so he prepared to leave for New Haven. Just as he was ready to quit Washington—on a train that left within the hour—Douglas had a call from President Roosevelt, announcing his appointment as the new chairman of the SEC.

8
The Making of
a Political Philosopher

Another man might have felt the chairmanship of the
Securities and Exchange Commission was a mixed bless-
ing. A few days after the appointment, the New York
Stock Exchange went into a decline that was almost as
serious as that of 1929. Many friends wanted Douglas
to close the stock market (which he had the power to do).
But he believed that if he did close the market, the whole
nation would believe thereafter that the SEC had destroyed the system. Instead, he let it remain open and
although there were alarming days, the market did not
collapse. The reason it had gone down so sharply, Douglas was later to tell Franklin D. Roosevelt, was that
Roosevelt had cut federal spending, and this action had
brought a crisis in confidence in the shaky business
community of the 1930s.

By 1936 President Roosevelt had taken Douglas into
his inner circle of advisors, a position he enjoyed into
the 1940s. Douglas was one of the ones to learn early
that FDR wanted to run for an unprecedented third

term. George Washington had set the precedent of two terms for a president, and presidents had followed that lead for nearly 140 years. But after World War II began in 1939, FDR could not conceive of relinquishing the office in the world crisis, and he decided to run again. Douglas was at the White House the spring day that Roosevelt casually said that the third term was on.

Douglas's influence extended beyond his appointive role. He had the ear of FDR, and that meant if he recommended someone for a post, that man was quite likely to get it. For example, through Douglas's influence, James V. Forrestal was brought from Wall Street into government as undersecretary of the Navy. Later Forrestal became the first U.S. secretary of defense.

The conviction of Richard Whitney, head of the New York Stock Exchange, on criminal charges, brought about the reorganization of the exchange under SEC management. That changeover, in 1938, marked the real gulf between the old ways and the new. Douglas engineered this change, and the financial community really never forgave him for it. Forever afterward Douglas was regarded on Wall Street as a raging lion (at best) or a revolutionary (at worst).

During these years with the SEC, Douglas and his staff were subjected to many temptations, attempts to bribe them, and attempts to bully them. That was natural enough, for the people whom they were regulating were the power brokers of the nation. At one time Douglas was in deadly battle with A.P. Giannini, the founder of California's Bank of America and one of the most powerful men in the U.S. Giannini conducted a campaign to discredit the SEC and its chairman.

On another occasion a delegation of important men of the financial world of Wall Street tried to intercede with President Roosevelt to have Douglas fired as SEC chairman. He was a dangerous man, they said. The president laughed at them.

FDR did not laugh, however, on another occasion, when Douglas revealed that the president's son, James Roosevelt, was involved in a scheme which might have made millions in profits for several people—all of it based on use of the Roosevelt influence. Douglas was nearly ready to resign over that incident, until Roosevelt made it quite plain that his son was a trial to him. Douglas, he said, was to proceed according to his conscience.

At this point in his life, 25 years before most Americans, Douglas already saw the need for "sunset" laws to eliminate unnecessary bureaucracy. Federal agencies tended to grow too close to the industries that they were supposed to regulate, he said. He proposed several times that all federal agencies should have an automatic cutoff after 10 years of life. Roosevelt disregarded the suggestion; it was only 20 years later that the need became apparent, and the 1970s before action came.

Douglas won some battles, he lost some. He lost a battle with Henry A. Wallace, the secretary of agriculture, over regulation of commodity exchanges, such as corn and wheat. Wallace said that regulation would hurt the farmers. Douglas also lost a battle with Jesse Jones, head of the Reconstruction Finance Corporation, a Houston financier whose agency used government money to back big industries.

In contests with Jones and Wallace and many others, Douglas observed the burgeoning of government and the danger of bureaucracy to personal freedom. Every major political figure in the Roosevelt administration wanted to enlarge his own area of authority in the federal government. This hunger for power worried Douglas, for although his enemies gave him many other uncomplimentary names, Douglas was always a "libertarian." He wanted maximum freedom for the individual, not socialism or other super-bureaucratic form of government.

But Douglas also saw in the American system grave dangers from unrestrained capitalism. He believed the abuses of big business had gotten America into the troubles of the 1930s.

As a student of law and government Douglas tested his theories of government. He worried about erosion of individual freedom, the basic guarantee of constitutional liberty, and he kept coming back to this point. He became friendly with Supreme Court Justice Louis Brandeis, and they often discussed the menace in the growing bureaucracy. Finally Douglas settled on one primary concern: the First Amendment to the U.S. Constitution, the guarantees of freedom of speech and press. Without these, he began to believe, all else would be lost. Government should exist for the benefit of the individual, and human rights must triumph over property rights.

As an intimate of Roosevelt's in the 1930s, Douglas was aware of the most confidential dealings of the administration. He was able to examine policies and make judgments of his own that would surface in years to come. He would write about these times in different ways in books. Most of his observations about government were based on his experiences at the heart of an administration that changed America more than any since Lincoln's.

Douglas did not like all he saw. He saw good ideas corrupted in practice, and the ambitions of his colleagues destroying much of what Roosevelt had set out to do.

But Douglas also concluded that government must maintain a large "public sector," which would exist alongside the private sector. He favored nationalization of the steel industry, so that steel production could be geared to public need, and not to the profit motive.

He also favored government employment of the unemployed, to relieve a serious national problem that persisted in resurfacing in all times of economic difficulty.

Douglas came to the conclusion that the Roosevelt program was not the revolution that had been hoped for, but a makeshift arrangement that did not resolve essential American problems. Later, he was to look at the Chinese Communist management of affairs on the mainland of China with considerable approval.

These ideas were shaped by the times and by many people. Douglas knew them all, from Missy LeHand, the

President's secretary, to Secretary of the Interior Harold Ickes, the professional curmudgeon of politics. Later, Douglas was to write about them in his gossipy autobiographical *Go East Young Man,* in sometimes amused, often respectful, and always tolerant manner.

He came, he worked, he saw, he learned. And then, in the fall of 1939 he was scheduled to go back to New Haven. Yale still wanted him to be dean of the law school. Douglas felt it was time to be moving on; he had no political ambitions. He was suffering from the disease of the public servant in the U.S. in those days—low pay. He had been working for federal government long hours and giving his job every effort for five years. And to show for it he had $25,000 in debts. Obviously something had to be done.

The only job Douglas really wanted in Washington was that of solicitor general of the United States. He was certain he was not in the running for it.

And so, in the spring of 1939, Douglas told FDR that he was going back to Yale. He was planning to leave for New Haven in June.

During these years in Washington, Douglas had become particularly close to Justice Louis Brandeis. The friendship began because Brandeis, who had delved into financial affairs himself as a young lawyer, was fascinated with Douglas's work at the SEC. And from Brandeis Douglas learned about prejudice, about the situation of the Jews in Europe. Brandeis showed him the evils of Naziism, when many other Americans were not yet aware of them. Brandeis's particular strength lay in Court matters that concerned the welfare and freedom of working people, and that appealed to Douglas, the small-town westerner.

Brandeis suggested to Douglas that government could be as lawless as a bank robber. He also impressed Douglas with his philosophy of government: that a public official held a public trust, and must be selfless in service in government. He taught Douglas new respect for old virtues that many another ignored.

For five years this association had continued. In the winter of 1938–39, Justice Brandeis told Franklin Roosevelt (never mentioning it to his young friend) that when he retired from the Supreme Court that winter, he would like to see Douglas appointed to his seat on the bench.

Brandeis sent his letter to Roosevelt on February 13, 1939. Douglas knew nothing about it, but Washington was full of leaks. At a party that same evening *New York Times* columnist Arthur Krock told Douglas he would be appointed to the bench.

Douglas paid no attention to the remark. He was too young, just over 40 years old. Further, Douglas knew that Roosevelt felt it was important to appoint a person from the Far West at that time. And although Douglas had grown up in Yakima, he had come east. He was a registered voter of Connecticut, not Washington.

FDR had made up his mind to appoint Senator Lewis Schwellenbach of Washington, to the Court, but he was dissuaded by some of the senator's enemies. Meanwhile, Douglas's friends were waging a furious campaign to secure the appointment for him. Arthur Krock was one. Another was Saul Haas, owner of radio stations in Seattle and other towns, and political-campaign manager for Senator Homer T. Bone of Washington, Schwellenbach's principal enemy.

Their problem was to persuade FDR that Douglas was a bonafide "westerner."

On March 19, Douglas was playing golf at a country club near Washington with some SEC associates. When they reached the ninth hole, a caddy came running up to tell Douglas he was wanted at the White House. He went into the clubhouse, changed, and drove to 1600 Pennsylvania Avenue, where he was admitted and taken to the Oval Office.

FDR was sitting there, grinning. He told Douglas he had a new job for him, "a dirty, thankless, mean job." And then he said he was sending Douglas's name to the United States Senate, as his appointment to the Supreme Court to replace Justice Brandeis.

It was the high point of Douglas's life.

The Douglas appointment was opposed by many liberals, in press and government. He was, they said, far too conservative for the job. This cry was taken up by the New Dealer, Senator Burton K. Wheeler of Montana, whom Douglas had earlier annoyed. The appointment was approved by the Judiciary Committee and went to the floor of the Senate. Wheeler and others spoke against Douglas. It was rumored that the principal labor leader, John L. Lewis, who was quarreling with FDR, would also come out against the appointment the next day. His open opposition might sway many Senate votes.

But Douglas's friends in the Senate managed a coup. They listened to the opposition speeches on the floor, and then they called for an immediate vote that day. Douglas was confirmed by a vote of 62 to 4.

And so, not knowing if he was suited for the judiciary, a little concerned because he felt he was getting into a job that offered no activity and very little excitement, William O. Douglas took his seat on the Court on April 17, 1939.

He was entering a whole new life.

9

The Judge Goes West

When William O. Douglas first came to Washington, the
Supreme Court of the United States occupied a little
room beneath the dome of the U.S. Capitol, flanked by
the halls of Congress. His old friend Justice Brandeis
had not even had a government office, as such. He had
worked at home, in an apartment he rented at his own
expense in the building in which he lived.

Just at the time Douglas was appointed, the new Supreme Court Building had been finished. It was a handsome marble structure on Capitol Hill, located between
the Senate Office Buildings, the Capitol, and the Library
of Congress.

Douglas moved into a suite of rooms that would be his
chambers for the next 36 years.

The tempo of his life changed. Suddenly he was
removed from the "main stream" of public affairs that
he had cherished, and thrust into the solemnity of the
contemplative judicial life. That way was accepted on the
Court in 1936. The Supreme Court justices had always

taken the view that men of the Court ceased to be as other men. The rules said they must hold themselves aloof from political life that coursed around them. They must be calm, collected, and totally unemotional in their approach to society.

That had been Brandeis's way. He believed in these rules and he functioned as one of the Court's most effective agents of change.

As for the Court, it was not far off the Brandeis mark in many ways.

In the beginning of Franklin D. Roosevelt's administration the Supreme Court justices were all "conservatives." Between January, 1935, and May, 1936, the Court outlawed several major features of President Roosevelt's New Deal.

Justices Roberts, Van Devanter, McReynolds, Sutherland, and Butler usually voted together, with others in dissent or not participating. These men were the conservatives of the Court. They decided that the National Industrial Recovery Act was unconstitutional. So were the Railroad Retirement Act, the Bituminous Coal Act, and the Agricultural Adjustment Act, they said. They outlawed the federal statute that provided relief for cities in the bankruptcy courts saying it violated states' rights.

In other words, the Court invalidated key New Deal legislation that affected nearly every American. The decisions hampered Roosevelt's efforts to change the economic structure of the American system, and create new opportunity through the "public sector."

Since these and similar decisions destroyed the effects of FDR's changes in the U.S. system, they outraged the administration. One columnist called the justices of the Supreme Court "The Nine Old Men." Roosevelt began to use that name.

The president planned to change the structure of the Court, which he could do only with congressional approval. In the early days of 1937 President Roosevelt offered legislation that would let him appoint one additional justice to the Court for each sitting justice who was 70 years of age or over. The plan was aimed directly at Justices Roberts, Van Devanter, McReynolds, Sutherland, and Butler. Supreme Court justices are appointed for life or until they decide to retire. In the case of some of those on the bench retirement might have caused hardship, for the justices retired on half pay.·

In all, if Congress approved, Roosevelt could appoint six extra judges. And if he did so, and appointed men of his own general political belief, the composition of the Court would be heavily weighted in favor of the Roosevelt social philosophy.

The New Deal had many enemies, in board rooms, in the halls of Congress, at the helms of newspapers and magazines. They called this measure a dishonest attempt to change the character of the Court while pretending to improve its calibre.

The opponents called Roosevelt's bill "the Court-packing plan." It brought forth acrimonious testimony in congressional hearings, and acidulous debates on the Senate floor. Finally—in July—the Senate killed the bill. Conservatives heaved a sigh of relief, and prepared to get on with the social and political war against Roosevelt and his New Deal.

The Court decisions seemed to change character. The justices of the Supreme Court had begun to read the newspapers, as one Washington wag put it. They seemed to see the immense support of the president by the American public. In the spring of 1937 the decisions of the Court began to be less restrictive than they had been in the previous two years.

Justice Roberts had been the first to change. He began to join Chief Justice Hughes and Justices Brandeis, Stone, and Cardozo in majority opinions (5-4 again) to uphold administration legislation that favored the broad reform of society. They extended the rights of women, and the rights of labor unions. They broadened regulation of interstate commerce.

Congress helped matters along with a law which allowed justices to retire at 70 on full pay.

In 1937 this law persuaded Justice Van Devanter to retire. He was replaced by Senator Hugo Black, a liberal southerner with whom Douglas had friendly dealings in the SEC days. Justice Sutherland retired six months later. He was succeeded by Stanley Reed, another liberal. Justice Cardozo died and was replaced on the Court by FDR supporter Felix Frankfurter.

In 1939 there were only two ultraconservatives on the Court, Justices McReynolds and Butler. In social and economic matters it was usually Hughes, Black, Brandeis, Frankfurter, Reed, Roberts, and Stone against McReynolds and Butler.

For several months, during the Brandeis vacancy, the eight-man Court had split on a number of issues, and so Chief Justice Hughes had scheduled a number of cases for reargument. These were among the earliest cases in which Associate Justice Douglas participated.

One case involved federal judges' salaries. In past years the salaries of federal judges had never been taxed under the theory of separation of powers. Congress had held that to tax judges would be to make taxation a political issue. Adhering to that same general principle, judges generally refrained from political activity, and even from voting in elections. They accepted the "outsider" role that society had thrust upon them.

Then came the case of O'Malley vs. Woodrough, which involved state taxes on a judge. The Supreme Court held the other way: it decided that a law passed by Congress in 1932 taxing judges' salaries was constitutional.

Douglas voted with the majority. When he cast his vote he decided that he was going to change the way that at least one justice of the Supreme Court lived.

He had been an extremely active person, and so when Roosevelt had said to him "you will hate this job" the president had not been more than half-joking. Roosevelt had expected Douglas to conform to the time-honored practices. But Douglas decided that he was not going to let being a judge keep him from being a citizen in every sense.

Douglas set out then to explore "citizenship" in ways that had not before occurred to him.

Because of the difficulty over his appointment (the big issue was whether or not he was really a westerner), Douglas took on the appearance of a professional westerner. He began to wear a five-gallon hat, of the sort that

ranchers and others in the livestock business wore. The
hat was a symbol to the world that William O. Douglas,
Yale law professor and SEC chairman of the past, was
really William O. Douglas, citizen of the West. From
that moment on, Douglas made no further efforts to
shake off the "rough edges" of the West for the sophisti-
cation of the East.

The change was more in style than in substance. The
yearnings for his Cascades had persisted in him through
all the years in the East. Whenever possible Douglas had
gone home for visits to his Washington country, or down
to Oregon where his wife had relatives. He spent as
much of the time as he could fishing and hiking and
tramping about the woods.

In the SEC days there had not been much time. But
the Court brought a welcome change. The Court recessed
in the spring and did not reconvene until late autumn.
The justices could go where they wished. Douglas now
gained the leisure to pursue the activity he loved. He
headed for the West.

10

Justice at Work

The appointment of William Orville Douglas to the U.S. Supreme Court had created a stir in Washington. Douglas was the youngest man appointed to the Court in 125 years, and that gave the press something to consider. Those critics who wondered if he was not too conservative for them were right in a sense. Douglas was really a conservative, and he so said. He was a conservative of the old school—one who conserved.

In those early days Douglas found his path in the actions of the New Deal. While others around him were shouting "pinko" and "radical," he was trying to help Roosevelt prop up a shaky capitalist structure that had failed to assure "life, liberty, and the pursuit of happiness" to millions of people who lived in America.

Roosevelt and Douglas were reformers who took the hard road of trying to salvage a system that some others said was not worth saving.

Douglas also believed that all men are born to be equal and that men should have the maximum right to pursue happiness in their own way. This attitude was a return to the old libertarian ideas of Thomas Jefferson and the revolutionaries.

In the cases that came up in 1940, Douglas was particularly active in writing decisions since many of the cases involved bankruptcies and finance.

But soon he found himself considering labor-union organization, and rendering judgments on matters that five years earlier he knew little about. The National Labor Relations Act of 1933 brought several cases before the Supreme Court. Some involved union busting. Some involved intra-union squabbles. Some involved union-organizing practices. Douglas's decisions were notable for their advocacy of the administration's policies.

It is not surprising that this should be so, considering the fact that, earlier, Douglas had participated in many meetings at the White House when these policies were under discussion.

Much later, three scholars made a study of Douglas's opinions in tax cases. They separated his judicial life into four major periods. In this period, 1939–43, Justice Douglas voted for the government in 82 per cent of the tax cases, and never dissented in favor of a taxpayer.

One major decision in which Douglas took the lead was that of the Sunshine Coal Company v. Adkins. It was to go down in legal history as setting precedent for the government of the coal industry.

The coal business suffered in the Depression years. The price of coal fell so low that many mines were closed. Thousands of miners were out of work. In the competition that struck the industry, big coal operators

cut prices and made special deals to force their smaller
competitors out of business.

Congress tried to control the price-cutting by an act
which was declared unconstitutional in 1936 by the old
conservative Court. When the nature of the Court
changed, administration leaders in Congress managed to
pass a new act regulating the bituminous coal industry.

The new act came before the Court in the 1940–41
term. The justices heard the arguments by the lawyers.
They discussed the case among themselves in their conference room. Each justice wrote his brief. Then each
justice voted. Eight justices agreed on a decision, with
Justice McReynolds alone dissenting.

Justice Douglas then wrote out for the public the
opinion of the Court.

What Douglas said, in essence, was that Congress had
the power to fix prices for the protection and welfare of
the public. Further, Congress could place the machinery
of price-fixing in the hands of public agencies.

The Sunshine Coal Company case set the pattern for
modern regulation of the U.S. coal industry. It was notable because it marked another blow at the old laissez-
faire capitalism. The Supreme Court's interpretation of
law put an end to a practice that allowed arbitrary wage
cuts by mine owners and brought hardship to a large
part of the industrial economy. This Supreme Court of
1940 showed a changed attitude toward the needs of the
American people. In many decisions, Justice William O.
Douglas was to be an important part of a judicial force
that impelled change and supported the changes
wrought by Congress and the executive branch of gov-

ernment, as the United States tried to find its way out of a depression caused by uncontrolled capitalism.

In the next few years, Justice Douglas would deliver so many of the opinions of the court that he would, in a very short time, make himself a lasting reputation as one of the sharpest minds and most effective social philosophers of his time.

11

Back to the Land

Mr. Justice William O. Douglas soon found it was good
to be a public figure; it was not so good to have to take
the brickbats thrown at him for his participation in the
New Deal, and later for his unorthodox views.

There were special rules of conduct to be honored by
a judge. He did not discuss court business with outsid-
ers. He did not campaign for political officials. He did
not become openly involved in any of the political activities of the executive branch of government. Such would
have been unseemly, and the latter might have been
illegal, given the separation of powers of the three
branches of government.

But Douglas was political none the less, and there was
talk in the spring of 1940, before FDR made the definite
decision that he was going to run for the third term in
1940, that William O. Douglas might be a man to watch
for the Democratic nomination that year.

In the summer of 1940 Franklin D. Roosevelt decided
he wanted a third term. Then he began thinking seri-

ously about the sort of man he should have as his vice-presidential candidate. It would not again be John Nance Garner, who was going to retire.

Some Roosevelt intimates said that Douglas had the inside track for the vice-presidency. Lawyer Douglas had amused FDR, but Justice Douglas had gained Roosevelt's respect for a new frankness and "toughness." Presidential speechwriter Robert E. Sherwood believed that Douglas could have the vice-presidential nomination that year.

But William O. Douglas was not the sort of politician that could scheme for what he wanted. When he could have been making contacts in Washington corners with "the right people," Douglas headed, in June, for Frances Lake in the Wallowa Mountains of Oregon.

Here on the Lostine River, Douglas later would build a summer camp, a log cabin of tamarack.

Several years earlier, Douglas had come to this country to a dude ranch operated by Roy Schaeffer who would become his good friend. Schaeffer undertook the management of the log cabin project.

Douglas had not been physically idle in these years in the East. He said that time and distance kept him too much from his Washington hills, but he hiked on the Long Trail, in Vermont and farther down after it joined with the Appalachian Trail and headed through the Berkshires, and crooked inland, all the way to Georgia. He had, in the Washington years, begun to investigate the beautiful Blue Ridge, with its spectacular scenery and its blue-gray, smoky sky. He went into Maine and New Hampshire, into the old mountains, with their second- and third-growth timber, and their rushing trout streams and little lakes. He took his children to the Maine woods and the shore, and taught them to love the out-of-doors as he did.

But now he began studying the management of the land, and he did not like what he saw. He began talking about wildlife preservation, and the saving of the timber lands, and the preservation of rivers and their aquatic life.

It was at about this time that Douglas began to write about conservation affairs in books and magazines. And in the early days at least, there did not seem to be anything very political about conservation.

On a fishing trip in the West, he joined a friend from the Fish and Wildlife Service. They decided to conduct an experiment in stream pollution. They caught a mess of trout, and kept them alive, and brought them down to the point near Portland, Oregon, where the Willamette River flows into the Columbia. They put them in a wire cage in the water.

The Willamette had once been a lovely stream, but by 1940 it was polluted by the sewage of Portland and other river towns, and by seven pulp mills, which threw their refuse into the water.

Those trout lived a very few hours in the cage in the oxygenless waters.

Douglas went out into the mountains to see what man was doing to his nature, and he came back to report on it in articles in magazines of every sort, from *Nature* to *Look*. In the 1930s he had achieved a certain reputation for his writings on financial-legal affairs, as well as for his government work. Now he became one of the most ardent and best known of western conservationists.

Soon the Lostine river had an even greater hold on the Douglas family. The children got horses. One day ten-year-old Bill came back from fishing to find a stranger in camp. They talked about horses and Bill admitted he yearned for a horse of his own. The stranger, Dan Oliver, gave the boy a horse. They named him Thunder.

A few days later, daughter Millie came up to the camp. She was stunned to find that her brother, two years younger, had been presented a horse out of the blue, while she, much older and more mature, had none.

Roy Schaeffer took pity on her then, and presented Millie with a horse. This one was named Lightning.

And so Lightning and Thunder came into the lives of the Douglases. They and many another four-footed equine were to make their ways into the family's hearts.

12

The Rights of Men

Douglas spent the summer of 1940 in the cool of the mountains, as Washington sweltered in the heat and at their Chicago convention Democratic politicians nominated Henry A. Wallace as vice-presidential candidate.

The election won, government resumed in the FDR pattern. The war in Europe, and the general feeling in America that it would spread, might concern a William O. Douglas as humanitarian, but these issues did not come before the Supreme Court. Douglas that year began to evince a strong feeling for limitation of the power of business over the individual.

One case, Olsen vs. Nebraska, involved exorbitant fees charged by employment agencies to their clients. The state of Nebraska had adopted a law limiting the fees of private employment agencies to 10 per cent of the first month's salary of the employee. The agencies went to court, complaining that the law was unconstitutional.

Not so, said Douglas, delivering the Court's opinion. Despite previous Court decisions that might be construed to indicate support for the agencies, the law was upheld. The Constitution, said Douglas, was a living document subject to reinterpretations.

In many decisions that year, Douglas backed the positions assumed by the Roosevelt Administration. It was natural enough, for Douglas was still close to those in charge of the executive branch of government. Some in Washington said he was closer than his colleagues thought proper.

In Washington in this period, Douglas became intimate with James V. Forrestal, who started his government life after a distinguished Wall Street career. They had met before, of course, during the Wall street days, but it was when Forrestal came to work at the White House that they became friends. And then Forrestal went into the Navy, as undersecretary for a long and useful government career. He and Douglas saw each other at least once a week, and spoke frequently on the telephone. They exchanged information and gossip about Washington, but their friendship was not widely known. It was not good for Supreme Court justices to be too closely identified with members of the executive branch.

And as for Douglas, his name was still anathema to many of the men of Wall Street, following his SEC days, and particularly the prosecution of Richard Whitney of the Exchange.

In these early years on the Court, Douglas struck out on his own. Justices had been aloof from the outside world. Not Douglas. He consulted often with Harold

Ickes and FDR and others about pet reclamation pro-
jects in the west, and the establishment of national parks
and the uses of public lands. He joined boards, domestic
and foreign, for the betterment of mankind. He began
to write and speak on public issues, largely matters of
principle and policies. He began to consider the problems of developing international law, so that it might be
more effective in control of the affairs of men.

The war years brought strains. There was difficulty
about securing gasoline, because of rationing. Travel
was not all that easy, and trips to the West, even for the
long Court vacation, were difficult to make.

Douglas, like most Americans, was restrained from
following his chosen pursuits during these years.

He was often considered for other tasks within the
administration. When it became necessary in 1942 to
appoint someone to manage war production, FDR leaned
towards Douglas, whom he admired for that "toughness" of spirit. But Douglas wanted no part of such an
assignment—he was not a production man, and he had
never engaged in business or industry. He wriggled out
of the appointment, and with enough finesse to keep
Roosevelt from becoming annoyed with him.

In 1944, Douglas was considered again for the vice-
presidency, but once again another was chosen—this
time Senator Harry S. Truman.

Meanwhile, on the Court, those nine justices were
rewriting judicial history, doing what author Robert S.
Allen called "hacking away the legal deadwood that had
accumulated since the Civil War."

For vast change had come over the Court. Chief Justice Hughes resigned. He was replaced by Chief Justice Harlan Stone, and the Court changed more.

Beginning early in the 1940s, the Court grew progressively younger (Douglas was the second-youngest justice ever appointed) and the young men brought new interpretations of the Constitution.

Yet even among these men, there were major differences. In the third year of Douglas's presence on the Court, he and Justices Black and Murphy seemed most often to agree on matters. And sometimes Justice Wiley Rutledge joined them.

Another faction was made up of Justices Frankfurter, Jackson, and Roberts, with Chief Justice Stone and Justice Reed swinging back and forth and often making the difference between decision and dissent.

It was not simply a question of "activist" or "passivist" views of the Constitution as some observers liked to put it, or a question of liberal or conservative, as others said. It developed from fundamental differences in the view of society and the law. And in this, progressively, William O. Douglas took the part of the small man and the individual against bigness and power.

Douglas's life on the Court was complicated, too, because of his close relationship with FDR. He was under pressure to give up the Court and return to the political arena in which he had fought so well during the SEC years. For although the SEC job was a cleanup campaign, it was also highly political.

In these years of the Roosevelt administration, Douglas was most often to be found on the side of the majority.

These years would be important years, but they would not be the most important for Justice William O. Douglas. His position on the Court would change soon enough.

13

Social Revolutionary

By 1945, Justice William O. Douglas had established himself on the U.S. Supreme Court as a practitioner of the tradition of "sociological jurisprudence." He was not interested in the legal technicalities of cases, which captured the attention of so many justices. Douglas was interested in the effects of the law on society, and above, all, on people as individuals. Many times, as he was considering a Court case, his mind moved back to days in Yakima, and on the road, when he had been chased by "yard bulls." Douglas had grown up a dissenter, and a dissenter he remained, unawed by wealth and power, unimpressed by "influence." He would rather be riding in a small boat down a rushing trout stream any day than cruising on the luxury of some millionaire's yacht in foreign climes. All this showed in the Douglas decisions and particularly in his dissenting opinions.

In 1946, President Truman tried to persuade Douglas to step down from the Court and take a post as secretary of the interior. Douglas had already acquired a reputa-

tion as a defender of the land. His fishing trips had
become famous. Washington reporters followed him out
to the West to interview him during the summer months.
He was in constant demand as a speaker on subjects of
public policy, and particularly of conservation policy.

Douglas turned Truman down. He felt that his best
place was on the Court, removed from the hurly-burly of
politics. From that vantage point he said he could probably do more good for the environment than he ever could
as administrator of a department of government.

Conservation needed friends on the courts. Oilmen, in
particular, were attempting to gain influence over the
land; the 1940s and 1950s saw a great effort on the part
of of the exploiter who wanted to milk the American
continent of its natural resources.

Douglas's involvement with civil liberties, too, began
almost immediately after his appointment to the Court.
One group often under attack was the Jehovah's Witnesses, an evangelical sect. The Witnesses infuriated
many other sects by their attacks on other branches of
organized religion. The resentment boiled over, to bring
them into Court for various offenses, most often concerning their proselytizing.

One case involved an attempt by authorities to impose
a municipal licensing fee on the Witnesses because of
their door-to-door practices. Douglas wrote the majority
opinion.

The tax was unconstitutional, he said, because it violated the Witnesses' rights under the First Amendment. This decision overturned a decision that had gone
the other way just a year before. Or, as Douglas put it:

"Freed from that controlling precedent, we can restore to their high constitutional position the liberties of itinerant evangelists who disseminate their religious beliefs and the tenets of their faith through distribution of literature."

In another important case, Douglas was with the majority of the Court, holding that compulsory saluting of the flag by children in school was unconstitutional.

One historic case dealt with freedom of the press. In 1946, Postmaster General Hannegan revoked the second-class mailing permit of *Esquire* magazine. He objected to its "lascivious" pictures. Evidence showed that the postmaster could cite only 86 of 1,972 pages of the magazine in 11 issues.

The second-class mailing-privilege regulations said the publication must disseminate information, or devote itself to literature, the sciences, arts, or some special industry. The Post Office contended that *Esquire* did not meet these requirements.

The real issue, however, was whether or not *Esquire* had gone beyond the bounds of "decency" in its "girlie" pictures.

In his opinion Douglas and the majority of the Court came straight to that point.

"The controversy is not whether the magazine publishes information of a public character, or is devoted to literature or to the arts. It is whether the contents are good or bad. To uphold the order of revocation would, therefore, grant the Postmaster General a power of censorship. Such a power is so abhorrent to our traditions that a purpose to grant it should not be easily inferred."

This decision had a lasting effect on attempts by various public officials to censor the press for "moral" reasons, an effect that continues today. The Douglas position is often cited by lawyers and judges in other cases.

So by 1948, Douglas was famous for his advocacy of the widest range of civil liberties. He and Associate Justice Hugo Black often found themselves together, and sometimes they were the only two justices on the libertarian side of an issue.

There were many challenges to the Douglas views. One came in 1947, when an employee of the U.S. mint named Poole was brought up on charges under the Hatch Act (which forbids political activity by public employees). Poole's service as a war executive committeeman of his political party had all been carried out on his own time, not the government's. Still, the government contended that Poole had engaged in political activity, and under the act, his behavior was a violation of the law.

The Hatch Act penalty was dismissal from government employment. Since 3 million Americans were employed by the federal government, the issue was important.

The Supreme Court held against Poole, and for the constitutionality of the Hatch Act.

Douglas dissented.

Poole, he said, was an industrial worker, and not in any way a policy maker. Nor did Poole have any connection with the mint's relationships with the public. The U.S. Civil Service was created to serve the government and the public. No one charged that Poole had taken government time or caused the government any expense, or in any way inconvenienced the government.

The government, said Douglas, was perverting its power, and corrupting its employees by making industrial workers "political captives," agents of a bureaucratic control. In that sense the federal government was guilty of furthering the aims of the party that happened to be in power in government at the moment.

Most Supreme Court judges seemed to have a talent for obscurity in their use of the English language. Or else they were prodigiously dull. Dissents like this one, phrased in such clear and expressive language, were understandable to lawyers, to reporters, and to the readers of the press. They did much to increase respect for Justice Douglas by lawyers and the public.

14

Challenge on a Mountain

Justice Douglas's professional life in Washington was busy. In the winter and spring the affairs of the Court took vigorous concentration. Even then he went hiking in the countryside when he could, exploring trails and ridges of the Virginia mountains, and the Maryland countryside. He discovered the old abandoned towpath of the Chesapeake and Ohio Canal that had once been a major traffic artery into Washington. He hiked along that towpath often, and introduced his friends to its delights.

When the Supreme Court was not in session, Douglas headed "for the hills." Although he was forty-seven years old, he undertook adventures that would have frightened many younger men. In the summer of 1945, he decided that he would climb Mount Adams, a 12,000-foot peak in the Cascade Mountains of Washington state.

He went west and met a group of old friends from his boyhood years on the Columbia River. They went down river to White Salmon, to begin the ascent of the eastern side of the Cascades. They moved then to the Trout Lake guard station, picked up a campfire permit from the Forest Service there, and went along the Forest Service road to Cold Springs, about 6000 feet in altitude, on the southern slope of Mt. Adams. They stopped there for the night; next morning the climb would begin.

Douglas and the others were up at 2 o'clock in the darkness, huddled around a small fire. They ate a breakfast of tea, soup, and crackers, and raisins to give them energy. In an hour they were on their way, each carrying a knapsack with chocolate and raisins in it, and a canteen of water.

In half an hour they found a trail that led up a ravine, and from that point on, it was climb, climb, climb. They passed an ancient field of black lava rock, and stopped at a creek to fill their canteens.

By five-thirty in the morning they could see the snow fields ahead. They were a thousand feet higher than they had been at the beginning of the day.

A number of the climbers—the young people—began to outstrip the middle-aged men, but Douglas's son Bill stayed with his father.

They stopped at 5:30, and found the air bitter cold, the wind blowing a gale around them. They could not see the sunrise because they were down in the bottom of a snow bowl, and to the east was a rugged outcrop of Adams that cut off the sunrise from their view.

Their route led up the south side of Mt. Adams. It was not the easiest side to go up, but neither was it as hard as the northside route along Killen creek.

The sun came up finally, as they climbed, but the wind

was blowing so hard they had to lean into it to maintain balance. And it was August.

Douglas discovered that, August or not, they had dressed too lightly for the occasion. They should have worn wool, and caps to cover their ears, but they were in light summer clothing, and soon he was chilled, and his fingers were quite numb from the biting cold.

When the sun touched them it brought no warmth, and soon, the wind blew away Douglas's western hat. Now his ears and face began to numb.

They climbed 2000 feet, and at 9000 feet reached a saddle of the mountain. By 10 o'clock they were on their first snow field, and after crossing it, they stopped for chocolate, raisins, and apple juice. It was a little warmer, for the sun was now high in the sky.

From here Douglas and his companions could drink in the magnificent view of the Western countryside around them. In front, to the south, was Oregon's Mt. Hood, and off to the west was Mt. St. Helens, both of them snowtopped. To the left was Little Mt. Adams and far above was Klickitat Glacier. It was volcano country; at some time 30 million years or so before, the volcanos had erupted here, and left that black residue of rock for man to see if he looked about him. Even then, sulphur fumes boiling up from the slopes of Mt. Adams reminded the climbers that the earth was still guardian of its mountains.

In spite of sun, as they plodded upwards along the ridge to the false top of Mt. Adams, Douglas and his friends felt the full force of icy wind that whipped through their light clothes and chilled them to the bone.

The younger crowd were way ahead of them, but they had expected that. They climbed up to the near-top without too much trouble, stopping, resting, and moving on. But the last 500 feet was grim going.

It was steep, in the first place. They were facing directly into the wind, and Douglas's upper legs were totally numb.

About half way up, Douglas began to wonder if he had gone "over the hill"—he feared he was too old to make so strenuous a climb. But with a little rest, his spirits revived. He struggled upward, step after step, until he reached the top, 12,307 feet above sea level.

Up on top was a wooden shack erected years before by the Forest Service. And here the climbers each year stopped and proudly put down their names, so their peers, the others who had made the arduous journey, might know them. Douglas and his crowd added their names to the list. Before them, he noted that only 20 people had made the climb that year.

Here the splendid scenery of the Cascades and the Yakima valley spread out below them, color and beauty on all sides, still virtually unspoiled by man, with glaciers and green fields and dark forests, and blue lakes.

Douglas felt that he had waited all his life for a chance to see this view of the country he loved. He said he would have liked to stay up there for days and days. But in fact, they began the descent in 30 minutes. The wind was blowing a 50-mile gale, and in their thin clothing they were threatened by many dangers. Not the least of these was the chance of being caught on the mountain at night.

They came down, heeling into the soft snow. Douglas and his son stopped and found the hat that he had lost in the cold of the morning. They moved below the snow line to timberline. They reached camp at 6 o'clock, hungry and tired, but pleased with themselves. For Douglas, dignified Justice of the U.S. Supreme Court, the climb was a new sort of achievement.

15

Disaster On The Trail

Given Douglas's temperament, the successful assault on Mt. Adams only whetted his desire to conquer. He dreamed of Everest—no one then had reached the summit. He knew that he would never climb Mt. Everest, for such work was not for middle-aged men who spent several months of their year sitting in overstuffed leather chairs poring over legal briefs. So he must be satisfied with less than Everest. But on Mt. Adams he had found his own answer to the question of why men climb mountains: it was a spiritual experience. And it could be repeated, and repeated.

That he would do. In the years that were to come he would climb Kloochman Rock, another of his boyhood dreams, and he would climb in Alaska and other faraway places, and he would journey to many lands, and look at high mountains from afar. Each year, as he moved farther afield, the spirit of adventure grew in William O. Douglas.

Not four years after the Mt. Adams climb, with many

adventures behind him, Douglas very nearly lost his life.

It was October, 1949, and he was starting on a horseback trip up Crystal Mountain near his Cascade home, with Elon Gilbert, a companion of many trips. They stopped on the trail to chat with Billy McGuffie, an old friend.

Then they were off again.

Douglas was riding a horse named Kendall, an animal he had taken on many mountain trips. But this day Kendall seemed balky. Douglas stopped and tightened the cinch that held the saddle on Kendall's back. He had gone about a hundred yards along an old deer trail when the horse shied. He reared and whirled around, turning and striking his front hooves on the slope.

Douglas slipped off over Kendall's tail, and landed on his feet. But he landed in shale, and the loose rocks slipped out from under his boots. He slipped, fell, and rolled downhill 150 feet, and stopped on a narrow ledge. He was unhurt and began to get up. Just then he saw an avalanche coming down on him. The horse was sliding. He came straight down on Douglas, knocking him flat, tumbled on down the slope to the bottom, and got up, without a single scratch.

But Kendall's rider could not say the same. Douglas felt his bones crunch under the half-ton weight of the horse. He tried to get up. He could not move. He lay on the ledge, paralyzed with pain.

He was alone, for Elon Gilbert had gone ahead when Douglas had stopped to tighten the cinch. He tried to call out. He could not even speak.

But Gilbert sensed the absence of any noise on the

mountain about him. He turned back. In 20 minutes he was there, to take a look and then hurry down the mountain to get help.

In an hour a rescue party arrived. The men lifted Douglas onto a litter and started down the mountain to a hospital.

Someone had called the state police, and a police car was waiting for the party at Chinook pass with an ambulance. Douglas was rushed the 60 miles to the hospital in Yakima.

To ease the pain, an intern in the ambulance gave him a massive injection of morphine.

But instead of putting him to sleep, it had another effect. He was allergic to morphine. The drug nearly killed him. He was unconscious most of the time for five days. When he awakened, he discovered that he had broken 23 of his 24 ribs.

For two months Douglas lay in the hospital in Yakima, flat on his back on a board. The mail began to arrive. There were hundreds of letters from wellwishers who had learned that Justice William O. Douglas had been seriously injured in a mountain accident.

For amusement, as he lay there, waiting for the damaged ribs to heal, he began to consider and turn over in his mind various developments in the history of man's search for human rights. Thus was born a project that eventually became a book—*An Almanac of Liberty*. But it would be a long time in execution.

At the end of two months, Douglas's doctors said they had done all for him that could be done at the hospital.

They suggested that he go to Arizona for convalescnce in the sun.

It was December. The Court was in session. But there was no question of going back yet—if ever.

When his body finally healed, many of Douglas's friends expected that he would live out his life as a semi-invalid. He would never ride a horse again, one doctor told him, and at first Douglas agreed. The thought of riding brought back memories of those horrible moments on the mountain. He was afraid.

Douglas was an old opponent of fear. As a boy he had a deadly fear of water, and had managed to conquer that only by forcing himself into deep water. He had done it, by himself. Now he told himself, he must force himself again.

So one day, he got up on a gentle nag that belonged to a neighbor. Immediately he broke into a cold sweat and began to shake. He got down, and went back to his house. But next day he was back again. He got on the horse, and dismounted, half a dozen times, with the sweat pouring from him, until finally he conquered his own fear. Then he began to ride the horse, and in a month he was going along at a full gallop.

The next summer, in 1950, Douglas was back in the Wallowa Mountains of Oregon. One day on a ride, he came to a bit of trail on a mountain that was almost the replica of the place where the horse, Kendall, had fallen on him. Again, sweat broke out on his brow. The panic returned. He steeled himself, but he knew that it might come back again. What would he do?

There were still worlds to conquer.

16

Endurance

Perhaps it was the suffering in the hospital bed and in the many months of convalescence, or perhaps it was the levelling and humanizing effects of life close to nature. Whatever the cause, in the 1950s, William O. Douglas moved back to basics in his attitude toward the law.

Returning to Washington, Douglas found himself immersed in one of the great political struggles created by the anti-Communist hysteria that struck the United States late in the 1940s, and held the nation in bondage for a decade.

In 1948, as part of its drive against Communist subversion, the Truman administration secured the indictment of eleven of the leading Communist Party leaders. The charge was conspiracy to teach the violent overthrow of the U.S. government.

The trial that followed lasted nine months, and was on the front pages of the newspapers day after day.

In this same period, wending its way to the Supreme Court, came the celebrated case of Alger Hiss, one-time

State Department official. Whittaker Chambers, a magazine editor, said Hiss had been a Communist.

The Hiss case had been conducted as a three-ring circus, beginning in an investigation by the House of Representatives Un-American Activities Committee. This case was more responsible than any other single factor for the rise of Representative Richard Milhous Nixon, an obscure member of the House of Representatives, to the presidency of the United States.

In essence: Hiss was asked in a Congressional hearing if he had once been a Communist. He denied it. Chambers identified him. Hiss denied knowing the man.

Hiss was tried for perjury in not admitting that he had been a Communist. The Hiss case caused arguments among friends and quarrels within families. Alger Hiss was convicted, and his name became synonymous with "Communist" and "traitor," and with dishonor.

When the case came to the U.S. Supreme Court, Justice Douglas said in the record of the trial that there was no proof of wrongdoing. No one accused Hiss of hurting the U.S. government. On the contrary, he had been highly respected in his years at the State Department.

Alger Hiss has risen high in the counsels of government. So high had he gone, in fact, that his very prominence worked against him. The Republiclans, in these years, were trying to "pin something" on the Roosevelt administration, and the Truman administration that followed it. By "getting" Hiss, they thought they had succeeded.

In the process of the trials (there were two of them),

Justices Frankfurter and Reed had testified as character witnesses for Alger Hiss. Thus, when the case came before the Supreme Court, they disqualified themselves as interested parties. So did Justice Tom Clark, because he had been U.S. Attorney General when the case was tried.

That left six justices to decide the case.

Only Justices Black and Douglas voted to hear the case. Had either Reed or Frankfurter been able to vote, they would, in Douglas's opinion, have had to vote to hear the case. And then the whole story of Alger Hiss might have been different, for Douglas never lost his belief that the entire affair was a matter of hysteria, contrived evidence, and political byplay.

But the hysteria was so high at this time that when Black and Douglas voted even to hear Hiss's arguments, they were subject to a campaign of insult in the press and even in the pulpit. Anyone who said that Alger Hiss might not be a traitor was likely to be called a traitor himself.

In this poisonous atmosphere, dozens of reputations were wrecked, scores, hundreds of careers were destroyed, and the brightest men of the State Department and other agencies were driven from government or forced to silence.

Many friends and acquaintances of Douglas's were driven to the wall. One was Owen Lattimore, a distinguished educator, writer and traveller. Douglas said Lattimore knew more about the Far East than any but half a dozen people in the world. Yet when Lattimore praised

the Communists of China, and criticized the National-
ists, he was indicted. He was "soft on communism." In
the 1950s that was a political crime.

In the midst of this period, the issue of the eleven
Communists of America came to the Supreme Court.
Specifically, it was the case of Dennis et al vs. United
States. Eugene Dennis was the secretary of the U.S.
Communist Party, and named as the major conspirator.

The case came up on June 4, 1951. The majority of
the Court held that the convictions of the Communist
leaders were proper. Justices Black and Douglas dissented.

Douglas pointed out that what the men had been
convicted of doing was teaching the works of Marx and
Lenin. Was that a crime?

As everyone in America knew, the Communist Party
was a tiny minority, and its members held virtually no
positions of importance in any segment of society.

Thus, said Douglas:

" . . . it is impossible for me to say that the Communists in this country are so potent or so strategically
deployed that they must be suppressed for their speech.
I could not so hold unless I were willing to conclude that
the activities in recent years of committees of Congress,
of the attorney general, of labor unions . . . were so futile
as to leave the country on the edge of great peril. To
believe that the petitioners (Communists) and their following are placed in such critical positions as to endan-
ger the nation is to believe the incredible.

"It is safe to say that the followers of the creed of
Soviet Communism are known to the F.B.I.; that in case

of war with Russia they will be picked up overnight as were all prospective saboteurs at the commencement of World War II; that the invisible army of petitioners is the best known, the most beset, the least thriving of any fifth column in history. Only those held by fear and panic could think otherwise."

But in spite of this plea for decency and the principles of liberty, the eleven Communists went to prison. Only much later did the truth come out, that the FBI had so harried the Communists for years that they were no danger to anyone at all. But that became apparent only long after Engene Dennis was dead, as were most of the others who suffered in the cause of their beliefs.

The Truman years were frightening years, for lovers of liberty. The Eisenhower years that followed were even more frightening. For where Truman had fought for freedom in his own way, Eisenhower did not understand or appreciate the principles involved.

There were, however, substantive issues that involved the national security, threats by espionage and subversive activity, and on the other side, the civil rights of all Americans.

One result of the second World War was the emergence of the United States as the world's most potent military power. The change caused worry in the Soviet Union about American intentions and certain aspects of American power. Since the U.S. alone had been able to build an atomic bomb, the Russians were particularly eager to get hold of any materials they could about American weapons. They began a thorough and effective program of espionage in the United States.

In the course of this espionage, a number of Soviet citizens were caught in compromising situations, and were sent back to the USSR. Proved spies were jailed or deported.

And many Americans were suspected of espionage. Some were arrested and tried.

In 1951, the FBI arrested Julius and Ethel Rosenberg and Morton Sobell, and accused them of espionage. They were tried, and convicted of conspiracy to transmit information about the atomic bomb to the Russians.

A judge sentenced Sobell to 30 years in prison. The Rosenbergs were sentenced to death. The judge, in keeping with the hysteria of the times, called their crime "worse than murder" and blamed them, in effect, for causing the North Korean invasion of South Korea in 1950; "Communist aggression in Korea with the resultant casualties exceeding 50,000."

On appeal, the Rosenbergs' attorney argued that the sentence was excessive. Never before had the death penalty been imposed in peacetime, in a civil court in an espionage case, and death sentences had been invoked in only two treason cases in American history.

The court said that the "cold war" had made of the Soviet Union an "enemy," and besides that the Espionage Act provided for death sentences for espionage.

The appeal was denied.

An unforgiving government prepared to kill the Rosenbergs. The Supreme Court, by majority decision, refused to interfere. Although Albert Einstein and the Pope tried to secure pardon for the offenders, President Eisenhower said the Rosenbergs were getting what they deserved and refused them executive clemency.

On June 15, 1953, four days before the day of execution, the Rosenbergs' attorney filed a petition of habeas corpus. A majority of the Supreme Court denied the petition on the grounds that all the issues had been covered, and adjourned for the summer.

That day, attorney Irwin Edelman filed a writ in the case, opening a whole new aspect: he contended that the Atomic Energy Act of 1946 superseded the law under which the Rosenbergs had been tried. He filed the writ with Mr. Justice Douglas, in the belief that he was more likely to get a fair hearing.

A Justice of the U.S. Supreme Court has the power to order a stay of execution while points of law are argued. In this case Douglas did so.

The action raised a furious outcry from the hysterical in America who were hunting Communist "witches." Douglas was excoriated in the right-wing press, and talk about impeachment was heard on Capitol Hill. But the execution was stayed.

Douglas justified his action.

" . . . I merely decide that the question is a substantial one which should be decided after a full argument and deliberation.

"It is important that the country be protected against the nefarious plans of spies who would destroy us.

"It is also important that before we allow human lives to be snuffed out we be sure—emphatically sure—that we act within the law. If we are not sure, there will be lingering doubts to plague the conscience after the event. . . . "

But the administration, and the surge of reaction in America would not have it so.

Attorney General Herbert Brownell petitioned Chief Justice Vinson to convene a special term of the Supreme Court to review the stay order.

It was done three days later. The justices were in a hurry to be away for the summer, the government was insisting that "traitors must be destroyed," and the whole matter did not take long.

The Court deliberated, and on June 19 voted to revoke the stay of execution Justice Douglas had granted. The Rosenbergs were executed the same day.

The unseemly haste with which this was all done provoked dissents from Justices Black and Frankfurter as well as Douglas.

Douglas was certain he was right on the law. And the law was all-important, for the intent of the Atomic Energy Act was to make less severe the punishment for crimes of this sort. The law said that the death sentence could not be invoked for what the Rosenbergs did, unless a jury so requested. And no jury had.

The Rosenbergs were dead by the time the dissent was published.

Representative W.M. Wheeler of Georgia put himself into the history books by the introduction of a resolution to impeach Douglas because he had "taken unto himself the authority to grant amnesty to two proven spies." This came in spite of the fact that the majority of the Court had noted that Douglas, feeling as he did, had an absolute obligation to do as he did.

Wiser heads prevailed, the impeachment move died, and the nation turned to other business. The justices scattered about the country, tending to their vacations. Early in 1954 the editors of the *Columbia Law Review* presented a disinterested study of the case. They decided that the complex issue of whether or not the Atomic Energy Act of 1946 superseded the Espionage Act had never been considered because of the "extreme haste exhibited by the Supreme Court" which had made it so that " . . . the rights of the Rosenbergs did not receive the precise and extensive consideration that must characterize the administration of the criminal law."

The Rosenbergs were dead, nothing would bring them back; and yet there were suspicions that Americans had been the major losers in the affair.

Douglas continued to fight what he believed to be injustice. One celebrated case arose from the long attempt of the federal government to deport labor leader Harry Bridges. Douglas took a strong stand against the "star-chamber proceedings" of the immigration authorities. Largely thanks to Douglas, twenty years later Harry Bridges was still in the United States, and on his retirement was hailed all over America as a "labor statesman."

From boyhood, Douglas had revered freedom, first the freedom of the out-of-doors, and then as he matured, freedom of the mind. In the 1940s and 1950s and 1960s, as he saw that freedom threatened in many ways, it was his inclination to fight against it with the weapons at his command.

In his many writings over the years, the voice of freedom predominates, whether it be the freedom of the big cat, wandering the open range of the far west, or the freedom of the little man from the oppressive power of the tax authorities.

As Douglas put it in one of his famous dissents:

"Law has reached its finest moments when it has freed man from the unlimited discretion of some ruler, some civil or military official, some bureaucrat."

Those are ringing words. They were fighting words in a Washington that was dominated by a love of the bureaucracy that amounted almost to a worship.

The most frequent charge against Douglas levelled by his critics was that he had rejected the austerity and detachment of a judge, to become a participant in the human struggle.

Douglas would never have denied that. His concept of the judges of the Supreme Court was as arbiters, not cold men in a cold room where the light of day and the noise of people did not invade, but arbiters of the law within the framework of an ever-changing society.

Early in his judicial career he had seen the importance of the dissent. He said the dissent in a court of last resort (the Supreme Court) is an appeal to the future, when a more intelligent or less personally involved set of judges, impelled by new knowledge and new attitudes, might correct the errors of a majority.

Justice Douglas also said it was the job of the courts to protect mankind from officialdom, to preserve liberty and, if necessary, to create new safeguards for freedom to apply in new times.

And to that end, many a time in the 1940s and 1950s came the message from the Court—an opinion had just been announced, with "Black and Douglas dissenting." That became a sort of watchword of those who loved freedom.

Freshman hazing at Whitman College. Douglas was hitting the water just as this picture was taken.

Graduation from Columbia Law School, 1925

Yale Law School Faculty in 1929. William O. Douglas, *top*, *right*. Robert M. Hutchins is in the bottom row, third from the right.

With daughter, Millie and son, Bill in
Astoria, Oregon, August, 1940

The Supreme Court on April 17, 1939. *Top row, left to right:* Felix Frankfurter, Hugo Black, Stanley Reed, William O. Douglas. *Bottom row, left to right:* Harlan Stone, J. C. McReynolds, Charles Evans Hughes, Pierce Butler, Owen Roberts.

Prairie House, Goose Prairie, Washington

17

The Traveller

Mr. Justice Douglas's fractured ribs healed with scars, and the lesions held his whole rib-cage like iron. He no longer had any expansion of his lungs.

So, said the doctors, Mr. Justice Douglas's outdoor life was ended. He had best stick to the inside of a cabin now, and even better stay at home in Washington, D.C., where he would be near doctors and hospitals.

But Douglas did not believe his doctors and he was quite determined to do for himself as an adult, what his mother had done for him as a baby. He had been paralyzed by polio, but his mother had rubbed life back into his legs, massaging them day after day, until some signs of life came back.

He had used those legs until he could march 40 miles across a mountain with a pack on his back.

So why not now?

Why not, indeed. Instead of quitting the outdoor life, Douglas chose in 1951 to make an expedition to the high Himalaya. He would not, of course, climb Everest. But he would climb mountains and he would see Everest. He began practicing a technique of deep breathing, bringing air up by pressing with muscles of the diaphragm.

Douglas went to India in the summer of 1951.

A United States Supreme Court justice was a personality whose travels were on the level of those of royalty of other countries. He was one of the handful of supreme governors of the United States, a representative of the highest level of the republican government.

So he was treated royally when he traveled in India. Douglas met Jawaharlal Nehru, prime minister and leader of the Indian government, whom he had encountered before in Washington. Nehru advised him on aspects of the mission into the mountains.

Accompanied by Indian guides, and sherpas, Tibetan mountain men, Douglas headed into the Tibetan plain for a test of his strength. For a solid week he lived at an altitude of 15,000 feet without oxygen. He made it; his deep breathing through the diaphragm worked.

In spite of the doctors, his mountain-climbing days were not over at all.

Before and after the mountain accident, Douglas had travelled widely around the perimeters of the Soviet Union. He wanted to go to Russia. But Soviet-American relations in the late 1940s and early 1950s were not such that a Supreme Court justice—a high American official—was very welcome in Moscow.

So Douglas travelled along the edges, learning about the USSR and its neighbors, and assessing for himself the political systems he encountered.

He was under no illusions about the nature of the

Communist expansion movement. Nor did he believe that Communists were "agrarian reformers." He referred to them as "practical politicians," who attempted to turn every local aspect of life to their own ends, including terror where terror seemed likely to work. But he also saw something that seemed to escape so many others: that Soviet Communism was a threat only where a political vacuum existed. In other words, in China the Communists triumphed against a tired and corrupt government. They threatened Persia and other areas of the Middle East, because there was no political competition.

Douglas began these wanderings with a little knowledge about the area, but an understanding of the nature of his own America, and the roots of freedom that were planted there. His detachment from the hysteria that was sweeping the U.S. also allowed him to see the nature of the threat to freedom, not the hobgoblins that were so often raised by politicians, military, and the press.

He went to Greece in 1949, when the Communist guerillas were still strong in the mountains of the north. He dined with Foreign Minister Constantine Tsaldaris, but he also travelled. He visited Greek Army battalions, but he also went to prison camps where he interviewed guerrilla prisoners. He argued about communism with Communists.

Where Douglas went he talked to people. He was entertained by governors, but he always sought out ordinary people to understand the workings of their lives.

In Iran, he went south to Mahabad, south of Lake Urmia. He met the Kurds, wild tribesmen of the mountains and steppes. He slept in Kurdish villages, and talked with the people. He ate with them, sitting around a low table, and eating with his fingers. He saw them dance. They talked politics.

He visited Lebanon. In Biblical days "the Cedars of Lebanon" were famous, but when Douglas arrived only a handful of forest acres remained in the whole land, and those high in the mountains. What Douglas recognized here was the evil of deforestation and overgrazing of lands. He stored these memories to write about at home.

He went to Syria, and he began to learn something about the Arab people. In the 1950s the Arabs were virtually unknown to Americans. A few oilmen were familiar with the region, but otherwise it was largely the realm of foreign correspondents. Almost no contact existed between the Arabs and America, except through oil. And the prevalence of Zionism had raised barriers against friendship.

With his son Bill, Douglas travelled to Jordan, and through the desert to Jerusalem. He wanted to visit Israel and learn how the Israelis lived alongside their unfriendly neighbors. The kibbutzim (collective farms) interested him most. In the early years these communal settlements solved many of Israel's population and labor problems. He was particularly interested in the Israeli reclamation of the desert, by irrigation.

When Douglas came back from his second trip, he wrote another book about that part of the world, *Strange Lands and Friendly People.* It was one of the first books to tell Americans in simple language just what one man had seen and what he had learned about other peoples. Above all, *Strange Lands and Friendly People* was an argument for humanity.

All this while, William O. Douglas was eager to get into the Soviet Union, to see for himself the nature of this "ogre" that was said to threaten the safety of the American people.

Even to apply for a Soviet visa in the early 1950s was bound to bring suspicion in many U.S. circles. Suspicion came also from the USSR. What reason could an American official have for wanting to visit the country? Since the Russians could not seem to answer that question satisfactorily among themselves, they did nothing. And so for five years, William O. Douglas waited.

Finally, in the spring of 1955, came a telephone call from the Soviet Embassy in Washington to the Supreme Court building. Mr. Justice Douglas's application for a visa had been approved.

By this time Douglas had travelled around most of the Soviet perimeter. It was like walking around a big box; he wanted to see what was inside.

But equally important, he was eager to see how the Soviet parts of the areas in Central Asia had been changed by socialism. As a patriot he was interested in seeing life under a totalitarian regime. As an adherent to the republican form of government, he wanted to know how socialism worked.

And as a judge, he wanted to see the impact of a police state on individual freedom.

So he approached the "Russian Journey" (that would be the title of the book he would write later) with almost boyish enthusiasm.

It was arranged for him to enter the USSR through Iran. Douglas took with him Robert F. Kennedy, third son of his old friend and benefactor, Joseph Kennedy.

Not many months before, Douglas and his wife of many years had divorced, and he had remarried. He would meet his new wife, Mercedes, in Moscow and she would spend the last days of the journey with him. But this early portion, which involved the outdoor life and camping conditions, was not suitable for her.

Douglas was not eager to be at the mercy of the Russians in the matter of interpretation. He secured permission to bring in an interpreter, but then the matter was caught up in the red tape of Soviet bureaucracy. The interpreter, Fred Flott, was unable to leave Teheran at the same time that Douglas and young Kennedy left.

The trip began on the dock of the Caspian seaport of Pahlevi. Here Douglas took passage on the Soviet ship *Pioneer.* On the twenty-six-hour voyage across the Caspian he taught the Russian captain and crew English, and learned a little Russian, and they laughed and smiled and had a marvelous time.

At Baku, Douglas and Kennedy got off the ship, and met their interpreters, a young man and a young woman from Intourist, the Soviet travel organization.

At Baku, they began visiting state farms. They saw sheep grazing with camels, on the sides of mountains that reminded Douglas of the American West. Wherever they went, they were feasted and the people outdid themselves to entertain the Americans. They toasted them in wine, and there were speeches and small talk.

The Russians wanted to show Douglas a favorable image. He was allowed to go nearly everywhere he wished. He was kept away only from the city of Leninabad in Uzbekistan and Karaganda in Kazakhstan. But where he travelled, no one balked at his questions, and he was allowed to see what he wanted to see.

The Douglas journey could not have been a great joy to the Soviet government. Wherever he went, it was not long before people were asking him questions about America. He responded, trying the best way that he could to set them right on the facts about the U.S.

The Russian people he saw believed that the Communist party in America was running ''neck and neck'' with the Democrats and Republicans. They did not know that the U.S. Communist party was a small minority (Douglas said 100,000 and he was giving the Communists all the benefit of the doubt) and that most Americans detested the party.

Then he had to explain why.

People asked him about unemployment, American unemployment being a favorite topic of the Soviet press. He explained the function of private enterprise in the U.S. He had to answer questions about lynching in the south, the refusal of the government to grant passports to a number of leftist Americans, and other questions of American policy that to the Russians seemed crude and inhumane.

Douglas told them what he knew, and he kept bringing up the subject of American standards of living, of cars, of housing—all of them so much higher than the Soviet.

He ate sheep's ears and sheep's brains, and drank camel's milk.

He was particularly interested in the enormous cultural variety of the USSR—so many different people from so many races and tribes. He was interested in the land, and how the people treated the land, in comparison to the way Americans managed. His book was a travel book, a political primer, and a report about what he saw.

He was interested in everything—in barbers, collective farms, housing and private plots of land reserved for workers. Douglas wanted to learn about everything, from the names of tractors to farming methods the Russians used here in this land so much like his own.

He wandered about with his Leica camera, taking pictures of people. He stopped on the streets of towns and villages to talk to people, using a Russian-English phrase book.

He was concerned with government, so he visited government offices and asked questions.

He was interested in Soviet agriculture, and surprised at the amount of mechanized labor he saw on the farms. He noted the absence (this was 1955) of hybrid corn strains in the USSR, and some of the failures of Soviet agricultural science.

He learned something about Soviet slave-labor camps (although most of this information came from outside Russia) and studied Soviet labor as much as he could. He was impressed with the freedom of American workers after he had seen conditions in the USSR.

Finally, as a judge, he spent as much time as he could discovering the facts about the Soviet police, the courts, and the law.

At Alma-Ata he interviewed the Russian Deputy MVD minister (state police) of Kazakhstan. He had personal experience with these police. They monitored his conversations, and checked his room at night while he was sleeping.

He discovered what a vast difference there was between Soviet and American justice, operating on different theories of law, in different sorts of courts, with different types of judges with totally different training.

He was particularly aware of the absence in the USSR of the writ of habeas corpus, the powerful weapon of the citizen against the state.

Most lawyers and judges of Russia, he sensed, had never heard of habeas corpus. The historians of the law knew it, but not the practical people. To them it was a "theoretical" branch of the law, this principle which Douglas described as man's basic guarantee of liberty.

Douglas saw some civil trials and some criminal trials.

Most impressive was a trial that involved a man who had stolen a woman's handbag. Douglas sat through the arguments, which were all standard. But he sat up and took notice at the prosecutor's closing remarks.

The prosecutor declaimed about the "sacred nature" of private property. And there was the great contradiction: people of the workers' state, practicing communism, still had a strong feeling for the rights of property. And so, in this regard, Douglas came away with the feeling that Americans and Russians were not so different after all.

The areas of freedom were certainly different. Douglas discovered that the Soviet people had no freedom of expression of the sort that Americans prized so dearly, but when Douglas emerged from the USSR he came out with the conviction that the Russian people and their government wanted peace (this was at a time when many Americans were not at at all sure of that.)

The death of Stalin had opened Russia in some ways to less repressive government. Douglas saw also what he believed to be the end of Russian clandestine operations in foreign lands with the death of Stalin.

Leaving the USSR, Douglas predicted a military stalemate between the USSR and the U.S. He predicted a vigorous peaceful competition between systems.

He came home sure that his own United States must turn to positive policies to help the peoples of the world, if the balance of freedom was to be maintained.

Those views were not totally acceptable in the America of the 1950s. Secretary of State John Foster Dulles believed more in containment of communism than in the pursuit of programs of economic aid abroad. And since President Eisenhower let Dulles mostly have his way, the Douglas position was attacked in Congress from the right. He got only lukewarm support from any but the most ardent liberals.

Douglas was dismissed in conservative quarters as a "lame duck" judge from the New Deal, and the "containment" of the USSR continued. It was nearly twenty years before his predictions about U.S.-Soviet relations were proved correct.

18

Freedom Fighter

In the late 1950s the U.S. Supreme Court changed.
Under Chief Justice Earl Warren, the court assumed a
liberality that President Eisenhower had never expected,
and apparently never wanted. Mr. Justice Douglas often
found himself cast with the Chief Justice then, although
one of them had been appointed by a liberal Democratic
president, and the other by a conservative Republican.
The cement that bound them was a love of freedom.

Douglas and Justice Black were alike, but different.
Black concerned himself far more with economics, and
Douglas devoted his energies to questions of liberty.
Perhaps that was because Douglas sensed that personal
liberty, and not economic welfare, was the burning issue
in America in the 20th century. The growth of bigness
in business, in government, in every aspect of U.S. society brought new threats to the freedom and welfare of
the individual.

Steadily Douglas gained reputation as the defender of
the rights of Americans.

Some of the cases were important because of the points of law involved. Some were important because of people.

One of the latter was the case of Rockwell Kent, the famous artist and writer.

Kent was politically on the left. He was unpopular with the federal government during the days of McCarthyism.

He had applied for a passport in 1952 to travel to Europe, and it was refused. The State Department accused Kent of being a "Communist," and of being guilty of "a consistent and prolonged adherence to the Communist-party line."

The government demanded that Kent submit an affidavit showing whether or not he had ever been a member of the Communist party. He refused. The government denied him his passport. He sued.

The decision was reached in 1958. In a five-to-four decision, the Court held that Secretary Dulles had no such right as to refuse an American citizen permission to travel abroad.

Douglas presented the opinion of the Court. In essence, it upheld the constitutional rights of the citizen against his government. The secretary of state had no right to withhold permission to travel from Americans because he did not agree with their beliefs or like their associations. It was as simple as that.

On that same day another case was decided, invalidating another State Department restraint on American citizens. The long war against the repression of the 1940s and 1950s was coming to an end, and certainly an important reason for its ending was the steadfast stand for freedom taken by a minority of the U.S. Supreme Court, which often meant Justices Black and Douglas.

On the Court, in the 1960s, Douglas's pattern seemed to be set—in behalf of personal freedom. In another sense, it was not set at all. For example, in discussing Mr. Justice Douglas's records in tax cases on the Court, that group of scholars who broke his record into four periods referred to the first as the Government Years— when Douglas had just emerged from the executive branch of government after service with the Securities and Exchange Commission. He was naturally close to Roosevelt, and his opinions tended to mirror those of his friend and patron.

That period ended in 1943. By that time Douglas had become far more independent. Roosevelt was bemused by the war, his interests had changed, his circle had changed too, and a distance had grown between the men. Douglas was much closer to James Forrestal, whom he saw or spoke with nearly every day. On one occasion he very nearly accompanied Forrestal to the Pacific to witness one of the major amphibious invasions of the war.

But on the Court, beginning in 1943, Douglas's sympathy had shifted to the individual, in tax matters and others. He had begun to see certain threats to liberty that had not appeared in the years when fear and poverty had been the enemy. With the coming of better times—even if they were war times—new problems arose, and government itself appeared in the guise of enemy sometimes.

That period, according to his legal critics, lasted until 1959. It gave way to what they termed the "extreme" period of Douglas's attitude in financial cases.

Quite probably this was his "extreme" period in other matters as well. He was very much the activist in every way, from his outspoken views on foreign policy (which embarrassed the Republican administration and brought him much criticism) to his growing feeling that personal liberty was at issue in America.

And then, in 1964, the students of Douglas on the Court indicated that they saw another change, to what they termed "tempered rebellion." That last is a good description of the Douglas career, for that is what he was, certainly by the 1950s and the 1960s, the "tempered rebel." He was in his 60s in *the* 60s, yet still a man with the spark of youth, who could still ride a horse all day long, and hike a mountain trail, and even climb a mountain.

In a way one could say that Douglas's best years were just beginning.

19

Political Analyst

Many men grow more conservative in later years, but Douglas grew steadily more concerned with freedom and the means of preserving it.

He had been to many lands in Asia. One of his books, *North From Malaya,* reported on his investigations of the difficulties in Southeast Asia. He saw then that the whole attempt to stop development of freedom and independence in Indo-China was doomed. The sort of independence the Vietnamese might have could differ widely from our own, but Douglas understood that the people there would not ever be content again to be under a colonial yoke.

He reached this conclusion early in the period when various experiments (as Bao Dai's rule) were still being considered as alternatives to Ho Chi-minh. But as Douglas saw, there was no real alternative to Ho.

On this trip Douglas visited a number of other countries. He was a good observer, and he had the fortune to have access to high officials that the average writer or foreign correspondent would not receive. Thus he was able, in relatively short time, to gather information that it might take others months or even years to come by.

Yet that alone was not the secret of his success as a writer about far-away places. Douglas had a nose for reality. He also had a fine sense of humanity, sharply honed from his own boyhood years. In the struggles of the peoples of Asia and the Middle East he saw much similar to the frictions between Eastern and Western Americans.

He visited Malaya, then immersed in a guerrilla war that virtually stopped the important rubber production for a time. He had the background after half a dozen years of travelling to make sensible judgments about what he saw. In Malaya—and this was the 1950s—he predicted that British policy ought to lead to a successful disengagement from the Communist revolution.

The British had learned the "secret." It was freedom. The British governors were actually preparing the people of Malaya for independence and political equality. That meant Malays, Chinese, Sikhs, and all others would be equal persons under the law and in the social structure. That is the sort of action it would take, Douglas sensed, to bring peace to any of these former colonial areas, where the white man had ruled so insensitively for so long.

As it turned out the British were right, and so was William O. Douglas. The Malayan experiment in democracy did work, and it did end the war, and bring into being a strong and stable government.

Douglas's way of getting information depended very

much on his way with people. This slender, middle-aged man with a ready, shy smile, and anything but the overbearing air of a public official, would sit down and talk to people. Where the languages were strange, of course, an interpreter would be involved. But Douglas had the rare quality of being able to communicate above the level of the interpreter. People sensed what he was saying, and the sincerity of his questioning.

One day on this trip he went to a Phillippine army camp not far from Manila. There he interviewed a young man, Tomas Santiago, who had been sent down from the hills to Manila by Luis Taruc, leader of the Hukbalahap guerrillas, to murder President Ramon Magsaysay.

The young man had begun his mission eagerly. He wanted to kill the president, because he had learned from the Communist guerrillas that the politicians of Manila were an evil lot, oppressing the people.

But on the road to Manila, something happened to Tomas Santiago, and he told Douglas about it that day.

He had been moving along the road, carrying hand grenades and pistols, with which to carry out his grim mission. He had reached Manila, and found Magsaysay's office. Then, two blocks away, he passed a group of Phillippine peasants who were talking. They had nothing but good things to say about Magsaysay. One told how he would punish any soldier who harmed a peasant.

Tomas Santiago knew the Philippine soldiers from other days. They were cruel men who killed many of his friends. So he argued with the peasants. They became very noisy. Some began to shout at him. Then one, who was an ex-Huk, recognized Tomas Santiago, and took him aside. He would make an appointment with Magsaysay for the younger man, he said. Let him see for himself.

So Tomas Santiago went into the office of the president, and he spoke to the man he was sent to kill. Magsaysay talked about what he planned to do to help the Philippines and the people, and Tomas Santiago handed over his pistols and asked Magsaysay to let him work for him.

But it was not to be so simple. First, said the president, Tomas Santiago must pay his debt to society. He must stand trial for the charges that the government had against him for his activity as a guerrilla in the hills.

Tomas Santiago did stand trial. He was given a prison sentence, but paroled to the custody of Magsaysay, and then he began to work for him.

That is what William O. Douglas learned in the talk in the army camp, and that is one of the stories he told in his book. There were many such stories, anecdotes that gave information and a sense of the place and time.

The book was successful. All Douglas's books of travel and adventure in his trips around the world were very successful. By the middle of the 1950s he was almost as well known as a writer of travel tales and on the subject of conservation as he was in the judicial field. He wrote books. He wrote magazine articles.

Some of his books came out of his work at the Court, books on freedom and the American adventure. The travel books represented a combination of reporting and scholarship.

Writing of his trips to Burma and Formosa and Korea,

he almost always said something about American policy
and the failure of Americans to understand what was
happening in the rest of the world, particularly in Asia.
For Douglas saw the challenge of colonial nations to
western society. He was not certain that the U.S. was
meeting it well enough. Indeed, he suspected it was
largely the other way.

It was a matter of ignorance, Douglas said, but because of that ignorance the Americans were squandering
the prestige we had built up in Asia over generations.

He wrote and made many speeches. He travelled over
much of the United States, speaking before audiences on
the subjects dear to his heart, and among them was the
opportunity of America in Asia—if we were bold enough
and not blind.

Douglas saw a world sharply divided. In the middle
of the 1950s he predicted that the Chinese Communists
would break their alliance with the Soviet Union. He was
hoping for the creation of a Pacific Union, something
like the "Third World," to operate within the framework
of the United Nations. His ideas were practical, and yet
philosophical, and anyone who read his works dedicated
to the study of the world and its affairs should have seen
that he was a far-sighted, patriotic man.

And yet such was the hatred in America in the 1950s
that many regarded William O. Douglas as "subversive." He was so called by the right-wing press. He was
insulted and attacked in many publications. Worst of all,
he saw his ideas basically ignored by the two Republican
administrations of General Eisenhower during this important formative period, the 1950s.

20

Young at Heart

The year 1960 brought another change to the life of William O. Douglas. John F. Kennedy was elected president of the United States, and Robert F. Kennedy, the young man Douglas had taken to Iran and to the USSR with him, became the attorney general of the United States.

So Justice William O. Douglas became an elder statesman in the Kennedy administration. As such, one of his major contributions was to make Americans conscious of conservation.

Douglas began to bring the out-of-doors into Washington. His particular vehicle for this move was the Chesapeake & Ohio Canal. Years earlier, poking about the environs of Washington on foot, Douglas had come across the canal. It had been George Washington's dream to connect Cumberland, Maryland, about 180 miles west, with Washington, D.C., and thus provide a necessary means of transportation in those days before railroads when Washington was president.

The first spadeful of dirt had been turned over by President John Quincy Adams in 1828. The canal was completed in 1850, and did its service for years, until the railroads brought their competition. Even then the canal survived, mules snorted and pawed and pulled the 90-foot-long barges along the towpath, until 1923.

When Douglas discovered the towpath more than two decades later it was overgrown and forgotten, an oasis, a sanctuary for wildlife almost in the heart of government Washington.

He came, fall, winter, and spring to walk along the path, admiring the beauties of the natural countryside that so few in Washington ever saw. He watched the blackbirds moving overhead in flocks, and he admired the magnolia in bloom, and the redheaded woodpeckers in the walnut trees.

Every time he walked here he saw something that had escaped him before, some delight of times past, times present, and what could be times future, but only if men preserved what was here from the ravages of a hungry urban sprawl.

He walked here often, and he began to write about what he saw. Had Douglas been of a different turn of mind he might easily have become one of the most popular of nature columnists for newspaper or magazine, for he had a way of describing all that he saw around him that brought interest to anyone who read. For example, in his book *My Wilderness, East to Katahdin*, he devoted an entire chapter to the towpath and the natural life of the area.

This was no short-time interest with Douglas. Once in

the spring he got together a group of nearly forty people, to make the 180-mile hike from Cumberland to Washington.

He had been doing such things for a long time. And as the years rolled on—the '40s, '50s, '60s—he became aware of the changes, frightening changes, that were moving all around him.

He noted that there were fewer and fewer robins coming to the area in the spring . . . and he discovered that DDT was cutting down the robin population.

And he watched the pollution of the Potomac, year after year. There was a day when John Quincy Adams used to walk down from the White House—or ride his horse—and go for a swim in the river before breakfast. But not in the 1960s. True, the days were gone when the fish used to come ashore and die, seeking oxygen destroyed by pollutants in the water, but the Potomac was muddy all the way.

Douglas took it upon himself to become a sort of keeper of the towpath, and frequently he took hikers—city people for the most part—on ten–and fifteen–mile hikes along the line. There might be a senator or two, and his wife if she was brave enough, and a cabinet secretary, and a newspaperman, and a dozen of Douglas's friends from odd places in life and country.

He wrote several books about the wilderness, at home and abroad. He wrote *A Wilderness Bill of Rights,* one of the most telling indictments of America's waste of our natural resources. He wrote a biographical study of one of the great naturalists of all times, *Muir of the Mountains,* —John Muir, the most powerful student of and tireless worker for the philosophy of Thoreau, and man's oneness with nature.

Douglas gave up hunting in favor of hunting with a camera and in the 1960s his conservation instinct was in full flower. The times were conducive to his writings. Beginning in the 1960s, Americans in many places were taking a new interest in the land. In Vermont, Oregon, and several other states, citizens groups and government began to study the impact of population on wildlife and natural beauty.

One of Douglas's boyhood heroes had been Gifford Pinchot, the forester. Now he began to pay back his debt to the past and to nature, many times over, by his leadership in the work of conservation.

Douglas did not forget those early days on the trail in the Cascade Mountains, with the fresh breath of meadow and forest in his nostrils. And during all these years he managed when he could to get back to this home country, where he would build his "home." He lived in Washington, D.C., most of the year, but he always wrote in *Who's Who* and other such directories that his home was Goose Prairie. For as he said, that was where his roots were buried, as they could never be in Washington. They were in Goose Prairie, that place not far from Yakima, which had so many memories. He bought twelve acres there, drilled two wells after "water witches" told him where, and got two fine ones, one for irrigation and one for the house.

He built a Swiss-chalet type of house, with a tall, pitched roof to shake the snows of winter. And around it he planted mountain ash, and dogwood, and azalea,

Oregon grape, and an old lilac bush that had grown up outside the window of his mother's house in Yakima.

There, in his private wilderness, he would go to observe the animals of his prairie, the deer and the weasels, the toads and the ground squirrels, the elk and the birds.

Goose Prairie had its grouse, its pileated woodpeckers, its hawks, and thrushes, horned owls—some 70 species he identified in all.

It was Douglas's haven, his place where he could retreat from the tensions of Washington. And here, in spirit, he was the youngest man on the U.S. Supreme Court.

21
The Controversial
Justice Douglas

The 1960s opened for Douglas in a way that was typical of his ability, in these years, to stir controversy. He had applied in 1959 for a passport to visit Communist China, and been turned down by the State Department. In 1960 he surprised many in Washington by advocating a seat for Red China in the United Nations. That advocacy won him publicity, but much adverse criticism.

In 1961, after the Kennedy Administration came to Washington, Douglas continued to be outspoken, particularly about Asian affairs. He advocated recognition of Outer Mongolia. He reiterated his call for Peking to take a seat at the UN, and predicted by 1967 Red China would be the third most important power in the world.

All of this brought public acclaim, speaking engagements, articles for magazines, awards, even honorary degrees. But beneath the acclaim, the boyish man remained basically unspoiled, a fierce defender of liberty, a staunch friend who did not forget his friendships, and a judge. If he was growing slightly less "activist" on the bench, he was heading now for the period in which he would be at his most judicial, and in many ways most effective.

When it came John F. Kennedy's time to select a Supreme Court justice to fill a vacancy, Kennedy did not turn to the liberals but to a conservative, Byron White, whose appointment swung the Court further to the conservative side, and made the Douglas opinions still more often dissents than in the past.

The appointments made by Eisenhower had shifted the balance; White's appointment strengthened change. The appointment of Arthur Goldberg, a liberal attorney, changed it back again, but only for a short time. The Court was growing steadily more conservative. Partly for that reason, the 1960s were very different years for William O. Douglas than any that had gone before.

There was too much to be done.

Douglas was where he had always wanted to be, in the middle of the stream of American life. One day he might be denying bail to Mickey Cohen, the infamous Los Angeles gangster. The next he could be appearing on a television program, speaking with enthusiasm about the new Peace Corps.

He became ever better known for his defense of civil liberties. He might be in Chicago one day, speaking critically of the Central Intelligence Agency's pattern of operations. (This was a good ten years before the criticism became general.) He might be in Cleveland the next week questioning the wisdom of local communities in trying to suppress "obscenity" in literature. He regarded such suppression as impingement on freedom.

Douglas had offers to leave the Court and take on new careers. His old friend from Yale days, Robert C. Hutchins, had secured an independent grant from the Ford Foundation to establish the Fund for the Republic. He became associated with Hutchins. The Ford Foundation indicated that it would make him a handsome grant to pursue his love of the out-of-doors.

One of his serious worries in the middle 1960s was the wave of conformity that had swept across the U.S. beginning with the McCarthy period. Douglas, the nonconformist, hated to see his beloved country losing its love for individualism.

Controversy swirled about Douglas. When his second marriage ended in divorce in 1963, some members of the Senate growled that they would investigate his morals. Senators regarded themselves as protectors of the Protestant ethic, apparently. When Douglas married again that year a girl who was forty-one years his junior, the event caused a new stir.

Supreme Court Justice or no, he was stricken from the social rolls of a number of Washington matrons. That was Washington society's way of showing distress and disapproval. It never bothered Douglas much, for his attitude toward Washington society had always been casual.

In these years the Court was fragmented. Douglas quarreled with Justice Black, most notably over the California-Arizona-Colorado dispute over the waters of the Colorado river. It was in a way the end of an era. For Douglas, Frankfurter and Black were the last of the Roosevelt judges left on the Court, and they had changed: the other two had grown more conservative, and Douglas had not at all—in many ways quite the opposite.

There was a good deal of public dissention among the justices in the 1960s, and it caught the attention of the press. There was also almost constant speculation that Douglas was about to retire from the bench—something he had no intention of doing.

He travelled everywhere, from Maine to Hawaii. And when he travelled he did not just go to make a speech. As when he spoke in Honolulu, he took several days and visited the outlying islands, to go hiking with his wife. He was interviewed on every subject, from civil liberties to fishing in Maryland.

Unfortunately, the third marriage lasted an even shorter time than the second. In 1965, Joan divorced him, and the next summer Douglas married Cathleen Curran Heffernan, who at twenty-three was forty-four years younger than her husband.

Douglas's enemies doubled their personal attacks. Within hours after the wedding one member of the House of Representatives called for a congressional investigation of Justice Douglas's fitness to sit on the Court. A Mississippi congressman demanded his resignation. Congressman Robert Dole of Kansas suggested that Douglas was not only an unreliable husband, but an unreliable judge.

And the rumors started over again. Would Mr. Justice Douglas quit the Supreme Court?

He considered resignation. He was upset by the bad publicity, and his independent spirit bridled at being the subject of public criticism. And yet he knew—there was no way of not knowing—that he had made of himself a public figure far beyond the usual, with his outspoken statements on matters of national interest and his travels and writings.

He decided to wait until the storm subsided. In a few weeks some other subject would seize the popular attention.

But within a matter of weeks Douglas was involved in another controversy.

Douglas's pay as a Supreme Court justice was $39,-500 a year. Douglas had never cared for money, but his travels and his divorces had been expensive, and he found himself constantly "strapped" for cash. For a number of years Douglas had lectured, and written books and articles in order to support his outside activities.

Some time earlier, the Albert Parvin Foundation offered Douglas $12,000 a year to join the board of directors. He accepted. The purpose of the foundation was to support fellowship programs for students from underdeveloped countries to attend Princeton University and the University of California at Los Angeles.

Other officials of the foundation were Robert M. Hutchins, Douglas's old friend, and Robert Goheen, president of Princeton.

A major asset of the foundation was an interest in the first mortgage of the Hotel Flamingo in Las Vegas. The connection (and the implication that this meant "underworld connection") was quickly drawn by the press, and the matter of "ethics" was raised.

A Republican senator wrote a letter to Chief Justice Warren asking his opinion of the behavior of his colleague, although no chief justice had ever passed on the behavior of another justice. The fire was burning once again. But once more Justice Douglas managed to wait until the attention of Washington moved elsewhere. He gave up the Parvin connection, but he insisted he had done no wrong.

In decision and dissent, Douglas was shoring up the foundations of American freedom. In one civil-rights case, involving conviction of 32 black students from Florida for peaceful demonstration (the charge was trespassing) Douglas dissented, holding that here was a violation of the First Amendment. A few weeks later he was dissenting again, this time in a case involving a matter of the right of privacy.

"We are rapidly entering the age of no privacy," the justice observed in his dissent, "where everyone is open to surveillance at all times; where there are no secrets from government. The aggressive breaches of privacy by the Government increase with geometric proportion. Wire tapping and bugging run rampant, without effective judicial or legislative control."

". . . The time may come," he added, "when no one can be sure whether his words are being recorded for use at some future time; when everyone will fear that his most secret thoughts are not longer his own, but belong to the Government; when the most confidential and intimate conversations are always open to eager, prying ears. When that time comes, privacy, and with it liberty, will be gone."

There was Douglas, crying out against government interference with human liberty. He was, once again, nearly a decade ahead of his time. Wiretapping and government invasion of privacy would really become issues after the Nixon abuses were made known, when Watergate had become an American word of shame.

In this period, late in the 1960s, the American public was splitting badly over the issue of the Vietnam war. Consistently Douglas held for the rights of the opponents of that war to speak out without harassment. Usually in these times he was dissenting again.

His health was good—a remarkable tribute to stamina, but he did have some problems. In 1968 he went into the hospital in Washington for implantation of a "pacemaker," a small electronic device that regularized his heartbeat. But he continued to exercise, to walk along the C & O Canal, to go hiking in the forest and woods when he could.

Again he was busy on the Court. One day in 1968 he dissented—alone—against the majority decision that made it a crime to burn a draft card.

He was at the house in Goose Prairie that September, 1968, when he was asked to stop the shipment of a group of reserve soldiers from Hawaii to Vietnam. A few weeks later the Court overruled the stay, and Douglas again dissented.

And the cases kept coming up to the Supreme Court as the government demanded conformity from Americans. A group of high school boys in Dallas, Texas, were barred from school by the principal because he objected to their long hair. They brought suit, and the lower courts upheld the principal. When the matter came to the Supreme Court, the Court refused to hear the appeal, which in effect said it agreed with the lower courts. Douglas dissented.

"I suppose," he said, "that a nation bent on turning out robots might insist that every male have a crew cut and every female wear pigtails."

He was 70 years old that year, and in many ways still the youngest man on the Court.

22

The Tenuous Years

In the spring of 1969 Justice William O. Douglas fell ill
with appendicitis and went to Walter Reed Army Hospital for surgery. A few days later he was back again in
his office, attacking the Tennessee Valley Authority because it was planning a dam that would dispossess hundreds of families—and wreck a perfectly good river for
recreation.

Douglas's enemies were still eager to "get at him" if
they could. And they would strike any way.

They found a new reason to attack him in the most
ridiculous manner.

President Lyndon B. Johnson appointed Douglas's old
friend and SEC protégé, Abe Fortas, to the U.S. Supreme Court.

Fortas had left the SEC for a Washington law firm
headed by Thurman Arnold, another Douglas crony
from Yale days. The firm, Arnold, Fortas, & Porter became one of the most prominent and successful of Washington legal groups.

After Fortas was appointed to the Court, suddenly a charge was made that as a lawyer he had taken a $20,-000 fee from a financier who was later imprisoned for stock manipulations.

On Capitol Hill, the Republicans began to raise the issue. They insisted on the resignation of Fortas. If he did not resign, they said, he would be impeached—and while they were at it, they would impeach Justice Douglas.

So for no reason at all Douglas's personal finances were questioned again. The press dredged up the Parvin matter and also a Douglas connection with the Center for the Study of Democratic Institutions (Hutchins's organization), which paid Douglas $500 a day for consulting work in 1968.

Every effort was made to make trouble for the justice. The American Bar Association was called upon to refer the matter to its ethics committee, and it did. Chief Justice Warren began talking of the need for a judiciary-conduct code, which was an indirect slap.

In the heat, Fortas resigned from the Court, and the Douglas enemies cried that Douglas should do the same. But Douglas had unfinished business.

One of the reasons for Douglas's resignation from the Parvin foundation was his discovery that the Nixon administration had ordered an investigation by the Internal Revenue Service (a trick for which the Nixon administration became infamous) to make a case against him.

Douglas had detested Richard Nixon from the day that the Hiss case first came to his attention, and he saw how the publicity-loving young California congressman was riding the "anti-Communist" issue to political success.

In the years that followed, Nixon had trod on the toes of many of Douglas's friends, in political campaigns, and in his particularly vigorous (many said vicious) campaigning for other Republicans throughout the land. Nixon never hesitated to tar the enemy with any brush at hand, and a Democrat was an enemy and therefore fair game. Douglas did not play the game that way himself, and he could not understand a man whose "instinct for the jugular" was his foremost characteristic.

So when Nixon became president, Douglas decided that he would remain on the Court, no matter what. He would not let this right-wing Republican have the pleasure of replacing him with another right-wing figure.

"The strategy," he said at this time, "is to get me off the Court. I do not propose to bend to any such pressure."

And he meant Richard Nixon's strategy.

Senator Strom Thurmond, southern Democrat turned Republican, tried to make a case against Douglas in Congress. Senator Edward Kennedy, youngest of the boys Douglas had known for so many years, defended him.

At this time, enemies and reporters opened every possible aspect of Douglas's life outside the court. Thurmond brought up the fact that Douglas wrote articles for *Playboy*, the "girlie" magazine that shocked many Americans. But what Thurmond did not say was that the articles Douglas wrote for *Playboy* concerned the out-of-doors, conservation of resources, and civil liberties.

One columnist charged that the only reason *Playboy* published the Douglas articles was to curry favor with the Supreme Court justice. Douglas, he said, had assisted them in their evil ways.

But other columnists came to his support.

Perhaps the smallest voice was that of Samuel Crowningburg-Amalu, a columnist for the Honolulu *Advertiser*. As a Hawaiian, he had a strong sense of the needs of the underdog.

"Justice Douglas," he wrote, "is just about the best and maybe the only friend that a very little man has now or has ever had on the Supreme Court of the United States. He has stood—and often time alone—between the little man and the near unconquerable avarice of strong government. When no one else would listen, the hope never failed that the ear of Justice Douglas might still be reached, and in many cases he was the only hope . . ."

Sammy Amalu was at that moment a convicted criminal, a prisoner in a Hawaii jail.

The Nixon attempt failed. The Bar Association ethics committee backed away from the problem. For the next year or so the press tried to tie Douglas to various activities of the Parvin Foundation, because Albert Parvin, founder, had once had something to do with a notorious gangster. The reasoning was obvious: Parvin deals with gangster; Douglas deals with Parvin; Douglas therefore is next to a gangster.

But the American public was not paying that much attention. The intent of the Nixon administration was obvious, and Douglas had his supporters in Congress and elsewhere. Not only in the prisons of Hawaii was he known as the last resort of the "little man."

The impeachment idea hung on in Washington, however. Such self-proclaimed moralists as House Republican leader Gerald R. Ford suggested that Douglas was unfit to remain on the Court. (At this same time, Representative Ford was taking favors from various businessmen, as was revealed much later, when he became president of the United States.)

Ford attempted to secure the impeachment of Douglas in the spring of 1970, but he failed to arouse interest. The Nixon administration brought out big guns. Vice President Spiro T. Agnew suggested that Douglas was unfit to judge because he "advocated rebellion and revolution."

The issue of the moment was Douglas's new book, *Points of Rebellion,* in which he defended the principle established by the signers of the Declaration of Independence, that men had the right to rebel against a government they found intolerable.

Points of Rebellion annoyed the Republican establishment that had settled into Washington with Richard Nixon's election. Douglas espoused the viewpoint of young Americans who rebelled against "the Establishment." Nothing could have been more calculated to bring down the wrath of the Establishment upon him. So the impeachment talk revived again in the spring of 1970. In the administration no one particularly liked to hear him speak out against the wiretapping and invasion of privacy by the FBI and CIA. The public then did not

know what Douglas was privy to as a Washington insider
—that the FBI and CIA had passed all bounds of decency in dealing with Americans.

He told a college audience in passing that his own
generation of Americans "is politically bankrupt." He
also warned that unless mankind changed its ways
(which he did not anticipate) it faced extinction in less
than a century. This was an extension of Douglas's old
views on conservation, but in the climate of the 1970s
it found a new and readier audience. Nixon did not like
it.

In the spring of 1970, the Republicans were particularly furious because the Senate had rejected two Nixon
appointees to the Supreme Court as unfit.

The right wing took out after Douglas, led by Agnew
and Ford. William F. Buckley, the right-wing columnist,
fulminated against the justice, largely on the basis of his
Points of Rebellion. Ford, speaking with great bravado,
said a majority of the members of the House of Representatives favored impeachment.

It was obviously another attempt by the Nixon forces
to push Douglas into resignation.

The House Judiciary Committee appointed a special
panel to investigate all the charges against Douglas,
which ranged from disapproval of his home life to his
politics.

Columnist Buckley attacked Douglas again and again,
for his articles in "a pornographic magazine," which
meant *Playboy.*

And while the fury rose around him, Douglas went
about his business, working at the Court, writing his

articles, and walking in the countryside. He would put on an old five-gallon hat (he still wore it as his Westerner's badge after all these years) and an old jacket and trousers, and go off along the C & O canal for an afternoon's amusement. Or he might be down on the Blue Ridge, looking across the Virginia skyline from a rugged trail.

All spring the fury rose. The columnists bayed after him, and the professional moralists of Congress read and approved. But by summer, the investigation had come up with nothing on which a charge of "high crimes and misdemeanors" could be based. Gerald Ford said the investigators weren't doing their job right, or they would have found plenty. Some of Douglas's enemies said the federal executive departments had hampered the investigation by refusing to give out information.

By this time Douglas was back in the West, enjoying a vacation. To do so, he had to find a wilderness cabin six miles from a road. Only here could he get away from the press. Anyone who wanted to see him had to hike in. Two young lawyers with a petition to the Court did so one day. The reporters were not that vigorous.

All the criticism heightened Douglas's determination not to quit under fire so that Richard Nixon would be beneficiary of his retirement.

The issue was resolved at the end of November, when the special House committee reported that there were no grounds for impeachment. Some elements of the press tried again to dredge up old issues—the Parvin connection—but the public was not interested.

Douglas called a news conference just before Christmas to announce that he would stay on the Court, to help fight for civil liberties.

The victory was sweet, and complete.

Even the press was stilled.

By this time Douglas and Thurgood Marshall, the first black ever appointed to the Court, were regarded as the major defenders of liberal causes. Nixon had managed to appoint three justices to the court, all of them as conservative in viewpoint as himself.

Douglas was still able to sway the Court in some matters, though, and in 1972 he found himself on the side of the majority in a landmark decision involving the right of defendants, rich or poor, to a fair trial. But too often Douglas found himself dissenting against the series of "law and order" decisions handed down by this new Court. He was joined sometimes by Marshall, and sometimes by Justice William Brennan. Generally, the tenor of decisions in 1972 was such that Douglas said he was concerned about the future of the "accusatorial system," which presumes a defendant is innocent until proved guilty. He said the system was under attack by the Nixon administration. Supreme Court justices are placed in charge of emergency appeals from various judicial circuits, which means the areas of the U.S. covered by various circuit courts of appeals. Douglas was in charge of the Ninth Judicial Circuit, the West Coast, which included California, the most populous state in the union, and one where many important law cases now originated.

In the summer of 1972 Douglas was in Goose Prairie

when the case of Daniel Ellsberg and the Pentagon papers broke. Immediately he was thrown into the middle of it when a lawyer approached him for a writ. He ordered a stop to the trial of Ellsberg until the fall when the full Court could review the matter of Ellsberg's unauthorized release to the newspapers of "secret" papers concerning the Vietnam War.

Douglas remained in the news. One day he made a speech in New York questioning the constitutionality of the American presence in Vietnam. In an interview with Eric Sevareid of CBS, Douglas told a story about the strange ways of politics that had almost meant a drastic change in his own career, and in the nation's direction.

In the summer of 1944, when FDR had been looking about for a vice-presidential candidate to share his fourth-term campaign, Roosevelt had written a letter to Robert Hannegan, the party chairman, at the convention in St. Louis. He listed two men who would be acceptable to himself. The first, he said, was Douglas. The second was Harry Truman. But when Hannegan got the letter he had it copied and turned the names around. Thus the delegates got the idea that FDR preferred Truman, and he was selected.

As for Douglas, he was not sorry about it, and never had been. He was happy on the Court, although he probably would have been willing to be "drafted" for the vice presidency. Then he would have become president, not Truman.

And what difference would that have made to Americans!

For one thing, said Douglas, he would never have dropped the atomic bomb.

How close then, had this man been to remaking the whole modern history of the world!

23

The Good Fight

If William O. Douglas had had his way, the United States would never have been immersed in the bog of Vietnam, which cost so many lives, and destroyed the credibility of a whole generation of Americans in world eyes.

On the Court, Douglas consistently attempted to do what he could to move the U.S. out of its entanglement. But with the changed nature of the Court, his was a lonely voice. He pointed out in dissent that the power to make war was granted Congress, and that anyone who denied that the Vietnam War was a war, was disregarding the facts.

But the war went on, the Court voting, often 7-2 (Brennan joining Douglas) in favor of the continued debacle.

Douglas's final marriage was a happy one. His young wife, Cathy, decided that she too wanted to follow the law, and he encouraged her. She attended American University Law School in Washington, and passed the bar examination, then began to practice. He was immensely proud of her.

Douglas's force on the Court now was felt largely in his individual rulings. He was called upon to rule often in cases involving liberty and he was uniform in his opinions in favor of freedom. He was also often alone. But in the spring of 1973, the tide began to change. The Nixon era was coming to its end, the disgraced president losing public favor every day. The Vietnam War was ending, and Americans now generally accepted what Douglas had been saying all along, that it had been a disgraceful adventure, bound to fail.

In the spring—on April 18, 1973—Douglas reached the thirty-four year mark in service on the Court. Washington rang with his praises. Chief Justice Warren Burger referred to him as "a strong, articulate individualist willing to blaze new trails whether in the majority or in dissent, but also willing to tread ancient paths of law."

The press that had disparaged him now could not say enough good about him, even some of the same writers who had cried most loudly for his impeachment or resignation from the Court only three years earlier.

Douglas was concerned with his overall impact on America, and he felt that his message was dual. First, he wanted to leave a legacy of civil libertarianism. Second, he wanted to call attention to the despoilment of America by people of the past and the need to protect the country—the land, the water, the very air—from spoilers of the future.

The honors began to come. There were testimonial

dinners and awards. He was named a commander of the Order of the Golden Ark by the Netherlands government.

That summer, Douglas and his wife went to China. As Richard Nixon was fighting his losing battle to keep the presidency, William O. Douglas was on a triumphal journey to Hong Kong.

The Douglases spent three weeks in China, travelling out of Peking. But then it was time to go back; the Court would sit in October.

That year, his 75th, Douglas became the man to have served the longest on the Supreme Court. The press became almost courtly in its adulation—a complete turnabout. Douglas, who had been under fire and whose head had been demanded so short a time ago saw his enemies confounded. The cry was going up for impeachment of Richard Nixon, and Spiro Agnew had been disgraced for his financial manipulations in public office.

It was pleasant to be the object of the love of a nation. The publicity was almost uniformly good these days, even though the Douglas decisions did not waver in their course. But the nation, not Douglas, had come full circle, and in the 1970s the American people, far ahead of the administration in office, were returning to liberal thought. Behind them were the days of anti-Communist hysteria, and jingoism. The chastening effect of the Vietnam War had been almost total, and all across America people knew that what they were seeing in the Nixon drama was something more than simple corruption.

To them, the idealism and steadfast purpose of Justice William O. Douglas now was like a beacon.

Newspaper feature writers began to come to talk to the Douglases. The sure sign of folk heroism—homely articles—told how he sometimes did the cooking ("Bill makes a very good chicken dish with lots of onions and garlic.")

In the spring of 1974, the first half of Douglas's autobiography was published. He called it *Go East Young Man.* He was intensely sensitive to his position on the Court, and felt that he should not in any way discuss in an autobiography personalities or even many decisions.

Also he was extremely reticent about his personal life after marriage. And these factors became apparent in the book; it was important for what it did not say as much as for what it did say.

He had made arrangements for biographers. His papers would be made available after his death and then they could write as they pleased about him. But while he lived he would not encourage any biographers, nor would he give them any special access. And as for Court affairs, they must await the end of the man.

Reviewers found the Douglas autobiography "peculiar" and not satisfying in telling them much that they wanted to know about Douglas. But that was all they were going to get, it seemed.

Life went on—spring in Washington, much of it devoted to the unravelling of the legal tangles of Watergate —and the downfall of the Nixon administration that summer; then autumn, and the reconvention of the Court. Douglas stood forth as always, for civil liberties and for conservation; they were the hallmarks of his Court actions in these years.

Then, on January 1, 1975, William O. Douglas suffered a massive stroke. He was vacationing in Nassau and was rushed back to Walter Reed Army Hospital in Washington. He recovered, but the stroke left him with weakness on the left side of his body, and in considerable pain.

There was talk that he would resign from the Court, but he wanted to stay on, largely because he did not wish to leave and let another known enemy, Gerald Ford, appoint a successor.

But more than that, Douglas knew that the sort of successor Ford would appoint would be in the Nixon image; Ford was perhaps even more conservative than Nixon in many ways. And, like any man, the justice would have preferred to be followed by someone of his own choosing, or at least of his own political and social leanings. That was the way it had been in his own day. Justice Brandeis had recommended him above all others, and his appointment had finally come to pass.

In March, 1975, Douglas was recovered enough to return to his office at the Court.

He was in a wheelchair now, and very weak, but his mind was unimpaired. Still, his body demanded attention. He went to New York seeking medical attention there from experts. Little could be done to restore his strength, and that was what bothered him most—his lack of energy.

His health was so uncertain that his attendance at the Court was spotty. Often when appearing on the bench he did not speak at all, and that was quite unlike the Douglas of old.

And yet, in 1975, when the Court closed for the

summer, Douglas told the press that he firmly intended to be back on the bench in the fall.

The press became critical again. Articles appeared accusing him of lapses of memory, and his prolonged absence from Court decisions (said his enemies) was interfering with the judicial process. So the clamor began again.

But by September it was apparent even to his friends that something was amiss, and he felt impelled to leave Goose Prairie for a tiring trip to Yakima, to rule on a case, so the press might see that he was able to make judicial effort still.

But the attempt raised more questions than it answered. When all the statements had been made, he sat, still, for nine minutes before speaking, and the spectators began to fidget.

The long nine minutes became a national cause célèbre, of the sort that editorial writers discussed pontifically.

But on September 29 he was back in his office in Washington in the conference room of the Supreme Court, taking his place. He was beginning his 37th term on the Court.

And he did participate, in all but a handful of decisions that fall. On his 77th birthday he dined with his friend Justice Brennan. Yet the speculation continued; it was an editorial writer's field day to wonder whether he ought to resign, and if he did not want to resign, whether he could be removed. Even Erwin Canham, editor emeritus of the *Christian Science Monitor* (who had been pushed into retirement) made a case for the compulsory retirement of Supreme Court justices.

In the winter of 1975–76, Douglas was not well. He was in and out of Walter Reed Hospital, suffering "fever." He was confined to a wheel chair.

And one November day it became apparent that it was no good . . . he simply could not stand the pace any more. Not even until after the 1976 election that might bring into office a man of his own party, and certainly one more suitable to choose his successor than the Gerald Ford who had tried to have him impeached.

So Mr. Justice Douglas resigned on November 12, 1975.

The press reversed itself once more to praise this man who had served so long in government.

Even the conservative columnist James J. Kilpatrick, who seldom had anything good to say for Douglas, called him "one of the unforgettable Americans of this century," although, of course, he also had to say that he was "in some ways the Court's greatest adornment, and in some its greatest shame."

But the howling for his head ended. He stepped back out of the center ring, into the shadows. He would work on the second half of his autobiography. He would go to Portland, Oregon, to seek relief from the pain that dogged him. He would go back to his beloved Goose Prairie. He would spend part of his time in Washington, scene of triumphs and tragedies, and oh, so many memories, of happy sunny days along the C & O canal, of mountains he had climbed and trout streams he had fished, of children and strangers and friends he had met and left all over the world.

He left behind him a strengthened legacy of American freedom, result of his many battles, many of them as dissenter, in behalf of the "little man." He also left behind him a strong tradition—grown in so short a time —of conservation and environmental concern. He had preached this long and arduously on university campuses and in his writings, and America had heeded. He could see that in the twilight of his life.

The months went by, and then came a sort of crown to many of his achievements. Congress began to move to set aside a portion of the Chesapeake & Ohio Canal as the William O. Douglas Hiking Path. It was a modest thing, and yet the salvation of those three miles from the ravages of industrial society summed up, in a way, everything that William O. Douglas's life was all about.

Bibliography

Some of the research for this book was done in Washington, D.C., in talks with Mr. Justice Douglas over the years. Much of it was done in various libraries. I am particularly indebted to the Sterling Library of Yale University, the Annapolis Public Library, the Library of the U.S. Naval Academy, and the Nantucket Atheneum for the loan of articles and books.

The bibliography of newspaper and magazine references to William O. Douglas is too prodigious to include in any biography. All of his own works are in some manner useful for stories or clues to his life and thinking.

I list here a few of the works that I found particularly useful.

Douglas, William O. *Of Men and Mountains.* New York: Harper & Bros., 1950.

————. *Strange Lands and Friendly People.* New York: Harper & Bros., 1951.

————. *Beyond the High Himalaya.* Garden City, N.Y.: Doubleday & Co., 1952.

_____. *North From Maylaya.* Garden City, N.Y.: Doubleday & Co., 1953.

_____. *An Almanac of Liberty.* Garden City, N.Y.: Doubleday & Co., 1953.

_____. *Russian Journey.* Garden City, N.Y.: Doubleday & Co., 1956.

_____. *West of the Indus.* Garden City, N.Y.: Doubleday & Co., 1958.

_____. *My Wilderness: The Pacific West.* Garden City, N.Y.: Doubleday & Co., 1960.

_____. *My Wilderness: East to Katahdin.* Garden City, N.Y.: Doubleday & Co., 1961.

_____. *A Wilderness Bill of Rights.* Boston: Little Brown & Co., 1965.

_____. *Go East, Young Man.* New York: Random House, 1974.

Allen, Robert S., and Shannon, W.V. *The Truman Merry-Go-Round.* New York: Vanguard Press, 1950.

Bernstein, Barton J., and Matusow, Allen J. *The Truman Administration.* New York: Harper & Row, 1966.

Countryman, Vern. *Douglas of the Supreme Court.* Garden City, N.Y.: Doubleday & Co., 1959.

————. *The Judicial Record of Justice William O. Douglas.* Cambridge, Mass.: Harvard University Press, 1974.

Hamby, Alonzo L.. *Beyond the New Deal. Harry S. Truman and American Liberalism.* New York: Columbia University Press, 1973.

Meek, Roy Lee. *Justices Douglas and Black.* A doctor's thesis. University of Oregon, June 1964.

McBride, H.E. *Impeach Justice Douglas.* New York: Exposition Press, 1971.

Wolfman, Bernard, Silver, Jonathan L.F., and Silver, Marjorie A. *Dissent Without Opinion: The Behavior of Justice William O. Douglas in Federal Tax Cases.* Philadelphia: University of Pennsylvania Press, 1975.

INDEX

167